WALKING
IN
THE LIGHT

WALKING IN THE LIGHT

DR. NEIL ANDERSON

THOMAS NELSON PUBLISHERS
Nashville

Published in Nashville, Tennessee, by Thomas Nelson, Inc.

Unless indicated otherwise, Scripture quotations are from *The New American Standard Bible*, © The Lockman Foundation 1960, 1962, 1963, 1968, 1971, 1972, 1975, 1977.
Scripture quotations designated NIV are from *The Holy Bible: New International Version*, © 1973, 1978, 1984 by the International Bible Society. Published by Zondervan Bible Publishers, Grand Rapids, Michigan.

Library of Congress Cataloging-in-Publication Data

Anderson, Neil T., 1942–
    Walking in the Light / Neil T. Anderson.
        p.   cm.
    Originally published: San Bernardino, CA : Here's Life Publishers, 1991.
    Includes bibliographical references.
    ISBN 0-8407-4386-6 (pbk.)
    1. Christian life — 1960– 2. God — Will. 3. Christianity — 20th century. 4. Anderson, Neil T., 1942– . I. Title.
[BV4501.2.A474 1992]
248.4 — dc20   92-41361
                                                                    CIP

Printed in the United States of America

2 3 4 5 6 7 8 9 — 96 95 94 93

Contents

Acknowledgments

For forty-nine years people have been building into my life. Books by authors I never met and tapes by people I never knew have all contributed to my life. I'm grateful for all the teachers that I have had over the years. I'm sure each has contributed something to this book.

I want to thank Dr. Robert Saucey, Dr. Lloyd Kwast and my pastor, Reverend Byron McDonald, for reading through the rough draft and adding valuable insight and making needed suggestions. I carefully chose these three because I respect them and know of their love for the Lord and commitment to the truth. Together they represent theology, missions and pastoral ministry.

I couldn't have finished this project if it weren't for my wife, Joanne, who typed the rough draft. As always, I'm thankful for a faithful companion who supports me and loves me enough to give me honest feedback. I appreciate so much the patience of my children, Heidi and Karl, who lost a little of their dad during some long days.

I'm deeply grateful for Dr. Bill Bright and Campus Crusade for Christ. It was through the early days of this ministry that I found the Lord. Years later, I was one of the hundreds who stood up for full-time Christian ministry at Explo '72 in response to a message by Dr. Bright. I was an aerospace engineer at the time. The foundation that was laid by Campus Crusade material provided solid guidance during my early Christian years. I especially appreciate the staff at Here's Life Publishers who have been so supportive.

Joanne and I want to dedicate this book to our parents, Marvin and Bertha Anderson, Chauncey and Alice Espe. We have celebrated your fiftieth wedding anniversaries. Thank you for staying together and standing at the top of our two families. You provided the love and moral foundation that made easy our entrance into the kingdom of God. You met our needs and provided the guidance we needed when we were young. Now that we have our own family, we look to the Lord for our guidance. You made that transition easy. We love you and we thank you for all the good memories.

*Does God communicate His will
to us? If so, how?*

1

CAN WE
REALLY KNOW?

In a telephone conversation a lady asked, "Dr. Anderson, my pastor says my favorite television evangelist is a false teacher. Is he right?"

At a ministerial retreat, a pastor stopped me and said, "Neil, I've been at this church three years, and here's the situation . . . " After finishing his description he asked, "Do you think God is calling me out of there?"

A seminary student stopped by my office and asked, "You've met with my girlfriend and me twice now. Do you think we should get married?"

Good questions. Important questions for those asking them. They all hinge on the answer to a much larger question:

Does God communicate His will to us? If so, how?

Each of these fine Christians was coming to me because of personal confusion about how God reveals His will today. Specifically, they did not have the assurance that He had given them the spiritual discernment to make the right decision. They were thinking that I, like the referee in a game, would make the right "call" for them.

A Reliable Guide

If what the Bible teaches is true, and I believe it is, then you

9

don't need me or any other more "spiritual" person to help you discern the spirits of the age or to find guidance in the darkness we are living in. In the first place, we have the Bible, God's Word, which the Holy Spirit will enlighten for us as we meditate on it, providing us with remarkably clear guidance in most areas of our life. And secondly, we usually can experience the direct guidance of the Holy Spirit in areas not covered by God's Word—if we meet His conditions.

That kind of personal guidance occasionally becomes apparent to us very early in life. I remember as a young child sitting in church listening to the minister and thinking, *I can do that.* Years later, at one of the church services I attended in the military, I left with the sense that God was calling me into ministry. I even informed my parents in a letter that I was considering becoming a pastor.

God Prepares Hearts

It is not uncommon to sense a call into the ministry at an early age. Yet in my case, the unusual part is that I did not become a Christian until four years *after* my military service. This raises the question, "Does God prepare hearts even before we belong to Him?" Again, if we accept God as sovereign and actively at work in the lives of people, we really must believe that. The apostle Paul alludes to it in Ephesians 2:10: "We are His workmanship, created in Christ Jesus for good works, which God prepared *beforehand*, that we should walk in them."

So where did I end up after the military? Despite my sense of His call to ministry I became an aerospace engineer. Was I now outside of the will of God, or was God using that preparation to make me a better minister later on? I'll let you ask one of my students for an answer to that.

After four years in the aerospace industry, I again clearly heard God's call. I left a successful career and attended seminary. Along the way I had the privilege of serving as a club director for a campus outreach ministry, then as a youth pastor, an associate pastor, a senior pastor and now a seminary professor.

I never applied for, sent a résumé to or personally sought after any of those positions. In each case, I believe God clearly led me. When I started my walk with God, I had no desire to be a senior pastor and certainly not a seminary professor. My own sense of giftedness and direction became evident as I grew in the Lord.

A Matter of Shaping

You see, when I left engineering school, I was sure that my education was finished. I had no desire to pursue any more formal education. As I began to mature in the Lord, my desire to read and learn increased. The Lord was shaping my life in ways that I never would have anticipated. Since then I have finished two masters degrees and two doctoral programs. Anybody who knew me in high school would have to acknowledge that as a miracle.

As a result of my experience, and from my contact with many Christians, I have come to deeply believe that God does sovereignly govern the affairs of mankind. He gently guides our steps as we choose to walk with Him. I believe in divine guidance. I believe that God wants to make His presence known in our lives and in our ministries.

Discerning Deceiving Spirits

Yet I also know that there are false teachers and false prophets in the world. People are paying attention to deceiving spirits. This should not surprise us, of course, for the apostle Paul wrote to Timothy: "The Spirit clearly says that in later times some will abandon the faith and follow deceiving spirits and things taught by demons" (1 Timothy 4:1, NIV).

Does this deception happen in Christian circles, or is it only the experience of the unbeliever? Unfortunately, I have abundant evidence that today we have an extraordinary level of deception going on even among believers. I have been helping people find freedom in Christ for several years, and hardly a day goes by that I do not talk to a believer who has been deceived. Many, believe it or not, are in full-time ministry or preparing for it. They are all Christians desiring to know and do God's will.

While my ministry was developing, I watched several of my Christian friends (some were actually under my teaching) drift from the faith and fall prey to the deception of false teachers. I saw their character erode and their morality deteriorate.

At a conference, a pastor handed this note to me: "This may be an unreasonable request, but would it be possible to talk to you privately? I am a pastor, yet I struggle with bizarre thoughts that I used to think were from God, and I'm consumed by lust."

I have listened to hundreds of parents tell of their children falling away. Others have told me about their spouses, relatives and friends being deceived. That's the kind of world we live in since Satan deceived Eve, though it seems the intensity of the enemy's attacks are increasing as the day of the Lord draws near.

New Age Influence

Though New Age religion is not new, what is new is how it has penetrated every level of society in the Western world. You think you are going to a helpful seminar on resolving conflict in the workplace, when instead you are introduced to New Age meditation techniques. Without spiritual discernment, even the best-intentioned Christian can be deceived.

Your teenage son or daughter may have to take a class in health, only to find the teacher espousing New Age medicine. Your elementary school child is frightened by an appearance in his or her room or terrorized by nightmares that you cannot explain. Later you learn of your child's exposure to the game Dungeons & Dragons, opening the door to demonic activity.

That's why we need to expose counterfeits before we are able to fully come to grips with the subject of God's direct guidance in our lives.

Thus in Part One of this book, we'll see how many of us are being led astray by counterfeit guidance.

Counterfeits Result in Bondage

I have counseled people who were once heralded as great prophets, but now they find themselves in deep spiritual bondage to the lies of Satan. Others believed they were guided by God but were actually paying attention to a deceiving spirit.

A pastor wrote: "I discovered that one of the older members

of our deacon board along with two other long-standing members of my church practice a form of spirit contact that sounds something like a séance. They told me that not all of the spirits one can contact are necessarily bad and that one had to consider the enduring nature of the 'good things' they brought, such as healings and messages from the other side."

At the same time, in our technological age, many misguided people are so oriented to knowledge and are so anti-supernatural, that they have reduced our walk with God to nothing more than an intellectual exercise. Thus we will explore the balance between Western humanistic rationalism and Eastern mysticism.

I will also analyze fear, since fear is a great strategy of Satan. Through his lies he paralyzes his prey in fear so that they cannot do the will of God. Fear and faith are mutually exclusive—they cannot both be guiding a believer at the same time. With the rise of Satanism and the advance of the New Age philosophies, we in the church must know the truth and exercise discernment as never before.

Seven Standards for Divine Guidance

Once we have established how counterfeit discernment and guidance operates in our day, we will look at seven standards of divine guidance in Part Two. I will attempt to address such questions as: What is God's will for our lives? How can we tell the difference between the "voice of God" and deceiving spirits? How do we walk by faith, and how does the Holy Spirit enable us to discern the true from the false?

One of the elements of the Christian faith I have had to learn is that, at times, God seems to veil His face. We cannot seem to get any answers to our most important questions. It is then, I have discovered, that we need to simply walk with God through the darkness, trusting in His sovereign will for us. Thus in Part Three we will focus on "Walking With God."

No Easy Answers

I did not write this book simply to set forth some easy-to-follow guidelines for knowing God's will. My purpose is to help you walk closely with God, which does require an understanding of how He guides. I will do my best to draw a fine line on issues that are clearly black and white in Scripture, but I will cover grey issues only in broad strokes. Some things will remain unanswered and seem ambiguous until the Lord returns. It is not God's will for us to know everything or to be omniscient, but to be truly dependent upon Him.

I cannot answer all the questions that I have in my own mind, much less yours. I am deeply sensitive to the possibility of leading one of God's lambs down a wrong path. After all, it is a bit presumptuous for any mortal to say how God guides. But my prayer is that you will keep an open mind and search the Scriptures with me.

Be discerning of what I have to say. The Bible is the only infallible source, not Neil Anderson or any other pastor or seminary professor. How presumptuous to think otherwise. That's why I have committed myself to God's Word, since it is the only reliable source of absolute truth.

I encourage you to "be diligent to present yourself approved to God as a workman who does not need to be ashamed, handling accurately the word of truth" (2 Timothy 2:15). If I help some of you stay on the narrow path of truth in your walk with God, I will be satisfied. If I help others get back on the path, I will be thrilled.

Part One:

Discerning the Counterfeit

*We'll find truth somewhere between
the extremes of Western rationalism
and Eastern mysticism.*

2

RATIONALISM
VERSUS MYSTICISM

While sharing with a college group, I could sense that one of the local heroes wasn't buying what I was saying. Rather than try to ignore him, since he was distracting the group, I asked what he believed. He said, "I believe in this," putting his arm around his girlfriend. "I only believe in what I can see, feel, hear and touch."

I asked him if he had a brain. "You better believe it," he responded.

"Have you ever seen it, felt it, heard it or touched it?" I asked.

"I know it's there because I can sense its effect," he said with confidence.

I said, "Look around, and you will see the effect of God's hand everywhere."

A timid soul from another corner of the room entered into our discussion, "I think it's silly to argue about what is true," he began. "I believe in all religions. I just close my eyes and God reveals Himself to me. We can all be one with God if we will just let our minds be enlightened."

Same classroom, opposite ends of the spectrum. Eastern mysticism was squaring off with Western rationalism. Two opposing ways of looking at life, both contrary to the Word of God.

To understand these diverse ways of thinking today, we need to see how they have developed. It shouldn't be difficult to see the god of this world in action as we trace the move away from a God-centered faith.

The Shift From God

Secular humanism grew out of the Renaissance when people began to focus more and more on the glory of humanity to the exclusion of the glory of God. Human reason and scientific innovation became the final authority of life, replacing God's revelation. Man decided he could live independent of God. This is the same old lie from the Garden.

Humanism's goal was to gain freedom from religious superstition and the authority of the church, but it contained fatal flaws. With God out of the picture, the universe lost its purpose, meaning and value. People like you and me were no longer seen as being made in the image of God but merely as the product of evolutionary forces.

The Western Mind

How did this translate into Western culture? In search of truth, the Western world resorts to observation and experimentation, a process known as *empiricism.* The Western world's educational system says that all that needs to be known can be learned through a scientific method of investigation. Then once that knowledge is gained, rationalism steps in. The information must be analyzed by a rational person in order to be of value.

Having been an aerospace engineer and having completed a research doctorate, I certainly can relate to this process. To the scientific mind, empiricism and rationalism are two sides of the same coin. Do the research, then make the analysis. To accept something as true, it must be systematic and fit the facts.

An example of Western thinking would be the belief that if A equals B, and B equals C, then A must equal C. It's hard for a person educated in the West to accept the fact that there are many educated people in the world who think differently. A person raised with a Hindu mindset would say maybe A equals C and maybe it doesn't.

Empiricism and Revelation

Now let's take this a step further into the Christian world. Many Christians feel that the general revelation of God in nature justifies looking at the world through the eyes of empiricism. They would point to such passages as, "The heavens are telling of the glory of God; and their expanse is declaring the work of His hands" (Psalm 19:1). And, "For since the creation of the world His invisible attributes, His eternal power and divine nature, have been clearly seen, being understood through what has been made, so that they are without excuse" (Romans 1:20). Since all truth is God's truth, whatever we discover empirically by observation and experimentation must be true.

It sounds good, but I have serious reservations. In and of itself, nature doesn't provide any answers concerning purpose and meaning in life; it must be explained by special revelation, the Word of God. Second, the scientific method of investigation, by nature and design, does not take into account the spiritual world.

The scientific method was developed in the natural sciences, which are, generally speaking, precise sciences. By that I mean that all physical substances can be reduced to one atom categorized in the periodic table of the elements. Given enough time and experimentation, almost every chemical combination could be analyzed and explained.

The social sciences, however, are not precise sciences. We cannot accurately predict how man will react in any given situation. What we research is man operating in the flesh. How can this provide definitive truth to the child of God designed to walk by the Spirit? Obviously, it cannot. It can only verify statistically what is, not what can or should be.

Limitations of Our Society

Without the authority of the Bible, our society treats the social sciences as precise sciences. For instance, a judge may appoint a court-ordered psychiatrist to determine a person's competence. I would ask, "What psychology does the psychiatrist adhere to?" He or she may not have a biblical view of man, and "science" varies greatly concerning the nature of man. There are scores of psychological theories. Each has some truth, but none are capable of an infallible judgment.

There's another limitation. The laws of nature don't apply to the spiritual world. You may be able to get full cooperation from people for research, but don't expect the kingdom of darkness to comply. Even God doesn't submit to our methods of investigation. We can't put Him in a box. This doesn't mean that the scientific method is wrong; it's just incomplete and insufficient to be a reliable basis for our faith.

Finally, our best reasoning is always biased because of our culture, education and personal experience. None of us is a totally objective observer. We all look at reality through our own knowledge and experience. Wisdom, on the other hand, is seeing truth from God's perspective.

We need to interpret research through the eyes of revelation. Research does not validate revelation; revelation validates research. Research sheds light on what is; revelation sheds light on why it is, what it should be and what it will be.

Our ability to reason is limited on three counts. First, we can never be sure we have all the facts. Second, we can never be sure we are perfectly interpreting the facts. And third, we can never be sure what the consequences will be after any decided course of action. Consequently, we need divine guidance. There is only one who is all-knowing. We will never know so much that we will no longer need God. In fact, I have found that the more I know God and His Word, the more dependent I have become. I believe Paul's words illustrate this great need:

> Where is the wise man? Where is the scribe? Where is the debater of this age? Has not God made foolish the wisdom of the world? For since in the wisdom of God the world through its wisdom did not come to know God, God was well-pleased through the foolishness of the message preached to save those who believe (1 Corinthians 1:20,21).

Eastern Mysticism

The Eastern world takes an opposite approach from the Western world, looking at truth more from intuition than from reason. Hinduism and Taoism are metaphysical, relying on mysticism for divine guidance. The Eastern mystic sees the mind as the problem. If truth is to be known, the mind must be bypassed. Listen to the words of Guru Maharaj-Ji:

> Ignorance is only created by the mind, and the mind keeps the secret that you are something divine away from you. This is why you have to tame the mind first. The mind is a snake, and the treasure is behind it. The snake lies over the treasure, so if you want that treasure, you will have to kill the snake. And killing the snake is not an easy job.

Mystic sects talk of a "new organ of perception" in man, another way of "knowing." Yoga refers to the development of a third eye which gives spiritual sight to the advanced yogi.

Other sects refer to "intuition," the "psychic self" or the "unconscious mind" as the means of perception. They say that the first step toward spiritual growth is to train oneself to ignore all messages from the mind. Next comes the tuning of one's "second organ of perception" to the "universal mind" or the impersonal "god of mysticism." Once attuned, the psychic self can bypass the mind and thus perceive reality directly. Attempts to erase the mind range from transcendental meditation to Silva mind control.

Most Westerners, however, are uncomfortable with throwing their minds into neutral, and Hinduism is too ascetic for the materialistic Westerner. So this is where the New Age steps in. It takes this unpalatable Eastern approach and makes it appealing to Westerners.

The New Age movement modifies this mindless approach by claiming that the mind is not being bypassed; it is actually the mind that is achieving "cosmic consciousness." They say that the mind creates reality. This is the basic teaching behind the Church of Religious Science. Ernest Holmes and other proponents of science of mind teaching believe that the supreme, creative power of the universe is a cosmic principle which is present throughout the universe and in every one of us. Science of the mind teaches that we are creating our own day-to-day experiences by the form and procession of our thoughts. They teach that man, by the way he thinks, can bring whatever he desires into his experience. And so we can begin to see the popular appeal of New Age thinking to the undiscerning person.

The Unifying Factors of the New Age

Recently I was preparing for a conference designed to reach New Agers. After reading several volumes, I was struck by the fact that differing religious and philosophical groups which previously had very little in common were suddenly finding unity under the New Age banner.

The New Age movement is not seen as a religion but a new way to think and understand reality. It's very attractive to the natural man who has become disillusioned with organized religion and Western rationalism. He desires spiritual reality but doesn't want to give up materialism, deal with his moral problems or come under authority.

Do you remember the snake Maharaj-Ji mentioned earlier? Well, there was another snake in the Garden. And all false religions of the world are nothing more than different humps of that same snake. It would only make sense that they would hold some things in common. I've discovered six unifying factors in New Age thinking.

The first is *monism*—the belief that all is one and one is all. It says we all swim in one great cosmic ocean. All human ills stem from an inability to perceive this unity. History is not the story of humanity's fall into sin and its restoration by God's saving grace. Rather, it is humanity's fall into ignorance and the gradual ascent into enlightenment.

Clearly, this is not the case. There is a definite boundary between the finite and the infinite. Monism is a counterfeit to the unity Jesus prayed for in John 17:21. That unity is possible only as we are united together in Christian fellowship. New Agers would seek unity without the Holy Spirit. We are to be diligent to preserve the unity of the Spirit (Ephesians 4:3).

Second, *all is God*. If all is one, including God, then one must conclude that all is God. Pantheism would have us believe that trees, snails, books and people are all of one divine essence. A personal God is abandoned in favor of an impersonal energy force or consciousness, and if God is no longer personal, He doesn't have to be served. God is an "it," not a "He."

Hinduism says, "Atman is Brahman" (The individual self is really the universal self). Occultists say, "As above, so below" (God and humanity are one). Satan says, "You will be like God" (Genesis 3:5).

How revealing it is, therefore, for New Agers to say, "We are gods, and we might as well get good at it." Their thought is, "When I was a little child, I believed in God. When I began to mature, I stopped believing in God. Then I grew up and realized I was God." That's like me saying, "When I was a boy I believed in Santa Claus. Then I grew up and didn't believe in Santa Claus. Then I grew up some more and I found I was Santa Claus!"

A third unifying factor refers to *a change in consciousness*. If we are God, we need to know we are God. We must become cosmically conscious, also called "at-one-ment" (a counterfeit of atonement), self-realization, god-realization, enlightenment or attune-ment. Some who reach this enlightened status will claim to be "born again." This is a counterfeit conversion. Their faith has no object, neither does their meditation, so it becomes an inward journey. To us, the essential issue is not whether we believe or meditate, but who we believe in and what we meditate upon. We believe God and meditate upon His law day and night. These seekers contemplate their navels.

The fourth unifying factor is *a cosmic evolutionary optimism*. There is a New Age coming. There will be a new world order with a one-world government. New Agers believe in a progressive unification of world consciousness eventually reaching the "omega point." This is a counterfeit kingdom and we know who its prince is. It's not hard now to identify the head attached to the hump of this snake.

Fifth, New Agers *create their own reality*. They believe they can determine reality by what they believe, so by changing what they believe, they can change reality. All moral boundaries have been erased by the metaphysical influence of Taoism's *yin* and *yang*, the ebb and flow of competing and complementary forces. There are no moral absolutes because there is no distinction between good and evil.

Sixth, New Agers *make contact with the kingdom of darkness.* Calling a medium a "channeler," and a demon a "spirit guide" has not changed the reality of what they are. This is the head of the snake, and they don't know it. They are in contact with the god of this world instead of the God of Abraham, Isaac and Jacob.

Recently I received a call from a lady who was concerned about the turn of events in a small group she was attending. It had started out as a rebirthing class attended by a group of supposedly Christian women. A woman in the group began to function as a medium, and they thought they were hearing from God. They recorded six hours of videotape and manuscripted the words into almost a hundred pages. In the six hours of taping, five different personalities can be identified in the medium. The group was convinced they were hearing from God, Jesus, the Holy Spirit and two angels.

The lady functioning as a medium was later identified as not being a Christian. In the tape her eyes roll back in a trance-like state. At one point a voice says through her, "It's going to snow here tomorrow." I'm surprised that when it didn't snow the next day, they couldn't see the snow job being done on them!

How can a thinking person professing to be a Christian consider this as anything other than demonization? But it isn't just lonely homemakers who are being deceived. We shall see as we proceed with our study of knowing God's will how this deception invades every area of society today.

The Middle Ground of Truth

The truth is somewhere between the extremes of Western rationalism and Eastern mysticism. I believe truth lies at the apex of a bell-shaped curve, between these two extremes as shown on the next page.

The Western world has a hard time with the fact that we can know all things and be nothing more than "a noisy gong and a clanging symbol" (1 Corinthians 13:1). We have a tendency to extol the virtues of theologians and apologists over lovers and soul-winners. Because of my engineering background, I entered seminary with one goal: I just wanted the facts. My approach to evangelism was to win arguments. I finally admitted, though,

Colossians 3:15-17	**Truth**		Ephesians 5:15-20
Word of God			Filled With the Spirit
	right wisdom knowledge	real power zeal	
Kingdom of Light			Kingdom of Light
Kingdom of Darkness	**Left Brain**	**Right Brain**	Kingdom of Darkness
"Always learning but never able to come to the knowledge of the truth" (2 Timothy 3:7).	reason cognitive task verbal facts language math linear	intuition subjective personal visual feelings art music spatial	"Led by various impulses" (2 Timothy 3:6).
Rationalism			**Mysticism**

that I wasn't winning many converts that way. Later I learned, "Knowledge makes arrogant, but love edifies" (1 Corinthians 8:1).

When I became a Christian, I charged up the Western slopes of rationalism. But as the truth became more real, I slowed to a crawl, like many (if not most) of my evangelical associates who had either stopped maturing or were progressing at a snail's pace. I didn't want to let go of my intellectual approach; I wanted to stay in control. Besides, I didn't want to be too real. Being vulnerable is risky.

When I taught evangelism, I asked my students three things to help them break down the barrier of Western rationalism. One, have you ever met God? (The question was a little more subjective than what they were used to.) Two, can you describe the experience? Three, how did you know it was God you met? At least 90 percent had a subjective answer to the last question: "I just knew it!" Is that wrong? Not if 90 percent of my students found assurance that way. It sounds like a confirmation of

Romans 8:16, "The Spirit Himself bears witness with our spirit that we are children of God."

Our Whole-Hemisphere God

Some researchers have suggested that our brains have two hemispheres. We are led to believe that each hemisphere functions slightly differently from the other as follows:

Left Brain	Right Brain
reason	intuition
cognitive	subjective
task oriented	relationship oriented
verbal	visual
facts	feelings
language	arts
math	music
linear	spatial

When God works through the church, He doesn't bypass our minds. And neither does He bypass one hemisphere for the sake of the other. We only have one brain and one mind. We have a whole-hemisphere God. Without Christ, the cognitive people are "always learning, but never able to come to the knowledge of the truth" (2 Timothy 3:7). Without Christ, the intuitive people are "led on by various impulses" (2 Timothy 3:6).

Neither the rationalist nor the mystic will ever come to Christ by reason or intuition. Jesus said:

And I, if I be lifted up from the earth, will draw all men to Myself (John 12:32).

No one can come to Me, unless the Father who sent Me draws him, and I will raise him up on the last day (John 6:44).

When you lift up the Son of Man, then you will know that I am He (John 8:28).

Jesus is the ultimate revelation of God. He is the truth. He draws both the rationalist and the mystic to Himself when neither leans on their own understanding.

When we receive Christ by faith, we are transferred out of the kingdom of darkness into the kingdom of light. Cognitive-oriented Christians strive to be right and search for wisdom and knowledge. The intuitive-oriented Christians are looking for reality and power and want to express themselves with zeal. When fact-oriented people start desiring reality and feeling-oriented people start searching for biblical truth, we will probably strike the balance that our churches need.

The sister epistles, Colossians and Ephesians, reflect this balance. According to Ephesians 5:15-20, in order to stop being foolish and know what the will of God is, a Christian is to be filled with the Spirit. The Spirit-filled person will sing and make melody in his heart to the Lord. But according to Colossians 3:15-17, the way to know the will of God is to let the Word of Christ richly dwell within us. The result is the same—singing and making melody in our hearts. It's not either/or, but both/and! Being filled with the Spirit and letting the Word richly dwell within us are really two sides of the same coin.

Lifeless orthodoxy is dead. The Holy Spirit doesn't just work in the right brain, and the Word doesn't dwell only in the left brain. There is only one brain and only one mind and only one God. The Holy Spirit will lead us into all truth, and the Word is a living reality. We must strive to be both real and wise, or we will not live balanced lives.

That balance is our goal—not just knowing about it, but experiencing it in our daily lives. If this truly is your desire, then would you pray with me?

Dear Heavenly Father, You are more than a good idea to me. You are my heavenly Father. I desire for my walk with You to be real. But, dear Lord, don't let my desire to be real ever shove aside my need to think. I acknowledge that You have told us to think so as to have sound judgment. I choose to think the truth and Your Word is truth. As I grow in grace, enable me to be a good witness to those who are lost in rationalism and mysticism. I choose to be sanctified in Christ so I can give an answer for the hope that lies within me. I shall not fear their intimidation, but as I sanctify Christ as the Lord of my life, may my walk with You always be made evident by the fruit of the Spirit. Amen.

Issue Comparison

Issues	Rationalism	Christianity	Mysticism
Identity:	product of evolution	child of God	god
Truth:	empirical	revelation	intuition
Guidance:	reason	Word and Holy Spirit	psychic
Eternity:	nihilism	resurrection	reincarnation

DECEIVING SPIRITS

A seminary student stopped by my office to tell me he was having difficulty getting to school on time. What should have been a five-minute drive lengthened to forty-five minutes because a voice in his mind kept telling him to turn at intersections. Not wanting to disobey what he perceived to be the "still, small voice of God," he was treated to a tour of the city almost every morning.

A pastor's wife, desperately needing the comfort of the Holy Spirit and desiring His leading, passively believed that whatever entered her mind was from God. She soon found herself bound by fear and plagued by condemning thoughts.

These examples underscore the wisdom of John Wesley's words:

> Do not hastily ascribe things to God. Do not easily suppose dreams, voices, impressions, visions or revelations to be from God. They may be from Him. They may be from nature. They may be from the devil. Therefore, do not believe every spirit, but try the spirits, whether they be from God.[1]

Satan Lies, the Spirit Leads

Martin Wells Knapp, co-founder of the Wesleyan Church, wrote the book *Impressions: From God or Satan, How to Know the Difference.*[2] Writing at the end of the last century, Knapp attempts

to distinguish between the lies of Satan and the leading of the
Holy Spirit. By quoting Hannah W. Smith, he offers this insight:

> There are the voices of evil and deceiving spirits who lie
> in wait to entrap every traveler entering the higher regions of
> spiritual life. In the same epistle that tells us we are seated in
> heavenly places in Christ, we are also told that we will have to
> fight with spiritual enemies. These spiritual enemies, whoever
> or whatever they may be, must necessarily communicate with
> us by means of our spiritual faculties. And their voices, as the
> voice of God, are an inward impression made upon our spirit.
> Therefore, just as the Holy Spirit may tell us by impressions
> what the will of God is concerning us, so also will these
> spiritual enemies tell us by impression what is their will con-
> cerning us, though not of course giving it their name.[3]

In that same work, Knapp also makes one major point clear:
"Oh, that I could write one message with the point of a diamond
upon the heart of every Christian. It should be this: Be sure that
the slightest impression upon your heart disposing you to do
Christian work has a divine stamp, and then obey it at whatever
cost."

We have this tension. We do need to be aware of deceiving
spirits, but we also need to heed the leading of God. There is a
battle going on for our minds: "The Spirit explicitly says that in
later times some will fall away from the faith, paying attention
to deceitful spirits and doctrines [teachings] of demons" (1
Timothy 4:1).

This was graphically revealed by the research for our book,
The Seduction of Our Children. Steve Russo and I surveyed
thousands of junior high and senior high students. One of
southern California's better Christian schools returned the following results from 286 high school students:

- 45 percent have experienced some presence (seen or
  heard) in their room that scared them;

- 59 percent said they have had bad thoughts about God;

- 43 percent said it is mentally hard to pray and read their
  Bibles;

- 69 percent have heard voices in their head, like there was a subconscious self talking to them;

- 22 percent said they frequently had thoughts of suicide;

- 29 percent have had impulsive thoughts to kill somebody, like "grab that knife and kill that person."

I realize that interpretation of this data will vary according to our world view. If we don't believe in a kingdom of darkness, then a natural explanation would have to be given for the battle going on in these kids' minds. In our culture, if a person is hearing voices or struggling with his thought life, it is assumed to be a psychological or neurological problem. But I have personally counseled hundreds of people who are hearing voices and most situations, if not all, have been demonic.

As I share with these tormented people that they aren't going crazy but they are under attack, they usually respond, "Praise the Lord, someone understands." It's freeing to know this truth, because if people are mentally ill for some neurological reason, the prognosis is not very good. But if there is a battle going on for their minds, we can win that war.

Who's Well and Who Isn't?

Mental health experts define a mentally healthy person as someone who is in touch with reality and relatively free of anxiety. From a secular perspective, every person harassed by deceiving spirits would be mentally ill. The secular counselor would conclude that the voices people hear or the images they see are only hallucinations. From God's perspective, it is the secular person who isn't in touch with reality. The spiritual world is very real.

I'm so glad that the greatest determinant of mental health is a true knowledge of God and a proper understanding of who we are as children of God. This means we don't have to fear anything; we have an eternal relationship with the creator of everything. We are free from condemnation since our sins are forgiven. Above all, we know that we are loved. So we, of all people, should be mentally healthy.

But let me quickly add that the opposite is also true. The

greatest determinant of mental illness is a distorted perception of God and who we are. That's why you'll find that most secular counselors don't like religion. Their clients claim to be religious, but they have a sick understanding of God and their relationship with Him.

While I would disagree that God could ever be the cause of mental illness, I do believe that we should avoid being one-sided in our approach. In treating our mental problems, we have a tendency to polarize—psychotherapeutic ministries ignore spiritual realities while deliverance ministries ignore developmental experiences and human responsibilities. Either extreme cannot adequately address mental illness. Our problems are never not psychological. There is no time when our minds, wills and emotions are not all involved. At the same time, though, our problems are never not spiritual. There is no time when God isn't present. We need a biblical view of reality. We have to contend with the world, the flesh and the devil. We are both physical and spiritual beings.

Because our culture has ignored the reality of the spiritual world, it is set up to be deceived. The secular world is turning to spirit guides for guidance and channelers for advice. The gullible public doesn't even realize that they are dealing with demons and mediums, and the church is only slightly more informed. Ignorant of Satan's schemes, many are paying attention to a deceiving spirit thinking it is God. We need to understand how Satan works in order to know how to defend ourselves against him.

Satan's Strategies to Break the Believer

Most people don't understand the true nature of one of Satan's primary strategies: *temptation.* Though Satan used a piece of fruit to tempt Eve, it was merely an object of deception. Every temptation Satan uses is an attempt to get us to live our lives independently of God. Satan attacks in the area of our legitimate needs. Then we have to decide whether those needs will be met by living independently of God or by living in the will of the Lord Jesus Christ. Paul answers the question for us: "My God shall supply all your needs according to His riches in glory in Christ

Jesus" (Philippians 4:19). Satan, the deceiver, tries to destroy this lifestyle of Christ-dependency and rob us of our peace.

Another misunderstood attack of Satan comes from his role as *accuser of the brethren*. The accuser of the brethren is determined to undermine our understanding of who we are in Christ. Everyone entertains thoughts like, "I'm stupid," "I can't," "I'm no good" or "God doesn't love me." If we believe these accusations, we will live defeated lives even though our victory is assured in Christ. Satan can't do anything about our position in Christ, but if he is successful in getting us to believe we aren't complete in Christ, we will live as though we aren't. We can fight this ploy of Satan by reminding ourselves who has the ultimate victory:

> Now the salvation, and the power, and the kingdom of our God and the authority of His Christ have come, for the accuser of our brethren has been thrown down, who accuses them before our God day and night. And they overcame him because of the blood of the lamb and because of the word of their testimony, and they did not love their life even to death (Revelation 12:10,11).

Neither temptation nor accusation is Satan's greatest strategy, however. If I tempt you, you know it. If I accuse you, you know it. But if I deceive you, you don't know it. Thus the primary strategy of Satan is *deception*: "[Satan] does not stand in the truth, because there is no truth in him. Whenever he speaks a lie, he speaks from his own nature; for he is a liar, and the father of lies" (John 8:44). Satan is determined to undermine the work of the Holy Spirit who leads us into all truth.

Over and over, Scripture teaches that we will be led in truth:

> If you abide in My word, then you are truly disciples of Mine; and you shall know the truth, and the truth shall make you free (John 8:31,32).
> I am the way, and truth, and the life; no one comes to the Father, but through Me (John 14:6).
> I do not ask Thee to take them out of the world, but to keep them from the evil one. They are not of the world, even as I am not of the world. Sanctify them in the truth; Thy word is truth (John 17:15-17).

When we put on the armor of God, the first thing we do is gird our loins with truth (Ephesians 6:14). The seriousness of not walking in truth is seen when God intervened in the early church by dramatically striking down Ananias and Sapphira. Why the severity of the discipline? Because they were living a lie. Peter asked, "Why has Satan filled your heart to lie to the Holy Spirit?" (Acts 5:3) It is crucial for believers to live in truth.

Obviously, God knows what the primary strategy of Satan is. He knows that if Satan can operate undetected in any home, church, family, committee or person, and get people to believe a lie, he can control their lives. That is the battle going on for our minds. That is why "we are destroying speculations and every lofty thing raised up against the knowledge of God, and we are taking every thought captive to the obedience of Christ" (2 Corinthians 10:5).

The Battleground

I believe that the greatest access Satan has to the church in waging his war for our minds is our unwillingness to forgive each other. We are so slow to surrender to Christ in this area, even though the consequences of unforgiveness are so great. Paul said:

> But whom you forgive anything, I forgive also; for indeed what I have forgiven, if I have forgiven anything, I did it for your sakes in the presence of Christ, in order that no advantage be taken of us by Satan; for we are not ignorant of his schemes (2 Corinthians 2:10,11).

Jesus admonished us to forgive from our heart or He will hand us over to the torturers (Matthew 18:34). The word for *torturer* is used throughout the New Testament for "spiritual torment." Bitter people set themselves up for personal torment. Paul and Jesus urge us to forgive. That's the pathway to peace.

Satan, the architect of torment, is also battling for the mind of the unbeliever:

> But their minds were hardened; for until this very day at the reading of the old covenant the same veil remains unlifted, because it is removed in Christ.... And even if our gospel is veiled, it is veiled to those who are perishing, in whose case the

god of this world has blinded the minds of the unbelieving, that they might not see the light of the gospel of the glory of Christ, who is the image of God (2 Corinthians 3:14; 4:3,4).

As I was counseling a deeply troubled young man, I asked him about his personal relationship with God. Realizing he had none, I shared God's plan of salvation. I asked him if he'd like to make a decision for Christ, and he said he would.

When he started to pray, his mind blanked out and I could feel the presence of evil in the room. I looked at him and said, "There's a battle going on for your mind. I'm going to pray and read Scripture. As soon as you can, call upon the name of the Lord." After about five minutes, one word at a time came out, "Lord . . . Jesus . . . I . . . need . . . you." The moment he said it, he collapsed in his chair. Then he looked up with tears in his eyes and said, "I'm free."

How are we going to see people come to Christ if Satan has blinded their minds?

We need to exercise the authority that we have in Christ and demand that Satan release those people whom he is holding so they can see the light of the gospel. We need to fix our eyes on Jesus, the author and perfecter of faith (Hebrews 12:2). We are deceived when our thoughts are led astray from the only legitimate object of our faith.

Cults talk about our historical Jesus, but they preach Him another way. He's not the eternal Son of God; He's just a good moral teacher. Those who believe that will not be led by the Holy Spirit, but by a deceiving spirit. And they will have a completely different gospel. It won't be a gospel of grace but a gospel of works. Notice how Paul clearly teaches this in 2 Corinthians 11:3,4:

> But I am afraid, lest as the serpent deceived Eve by his craftiness, your minds should be led astray from the simplicity and purity of devotion to Christ. For if one comes and preaches another Jesus whom we have not preached, or you receive a different spirit which you have not received, or a different gospel which you have not accepted, you bear this beautifully.

Choosing Truth

It is our responsibility to use our minds and to know the truth:

> [We are] to think so as to have sound judgment (Romans 12:3).
> Brethren, do not be children in your thinking; yet in evil be babes, but in your thinking be mature (1 Corinthians 14:20).
> Therefore, gird your minds for action (1 Peter 1:13).

Passively putting our minds in neutral invites spiritual disaster. We are to choose truth aggressively and actively. The Magna Carta of this concept is found in Philippians 4:8,9:

> Finally, brethren, whatever is true, whatever is honorable, whatever is right, whatever is pure, whatever is lovely, whatever is of good repute, if there is any excellence and if anything worthy of praise, let your mind dwell on these things. The things you have learned and received and heard and seen in me, practice these things; and the God of peace shall be with you.

Don't pay attention to deceiving spirits. If a thought comes to your mind, compare it with the list in Philippians 4:8 above. Don't entertain thoughts that are contrary to it. Then follow the admonition of the next verse (verse 9), and put into practice what you know to be true. If we really believe the truth, we will do what we know to be right.

When I counsel people who are in deep spiritual conflict, I aim for two results. First, I want them to know who they are as children of God. Second, I want them to experience freedom and peace in their minds. With this desire, I sought to help a missionary who was struggling just to hold her life together. After our counseling session, she sent me this letter:

> The edge of tension and irritation is gone. I feel so free. The Bible has been really exciting, stimulating and more understandable than ever before. I am no longer bound by accusations, doubts, thoughts of suicide, murder or other harm that comes straight from hell into my head. There is a serenity in my mind and spirit, a clarity of consciousness that is profound. I've been set free. My ability to process things has increased many fold. Not only is my spirit more serene, my head is

actually clearer. It's easier to make connections and integrate things now. It seems like everything is easier to understand now.

My relationship with God has changed significantly. For eight years, I felt He was distant from me. I was desperately crying out to Him to set me free, to release me from the bondage I was in. I wanted so badly to meet with Him, to know His presence with me again. I needed to know Him as a friend and companion, not as the distant authority figure He had become in my mind and experience.

Now that I am free in Christ, I have seen my ability to trust grow and my ability to be honest with Him increase greatly. I really am experiencing the spiritual growth I had been praying for.

I don't know of a person who would not want to know that kind of freedom, joy and closeness to God. Isn't this your desire? To put an end to Satan's deception and be freed from his battle for control in your life? Or maybe you just want to reaffirm your freedom in Christ. Then would you pray with me?

Dear Heavenly Father, I thank You for setting the captives free. I have accepted Your free gift of salvation, so I am now a child of God, seated with Christ in the heavenlies. I know that nothing can separate me from Your love or snatch me out of Your hand. Your Holy Spirit bears witness to me that I am Your child.

I bring my anxious thoughts before You and ask that Your peace would guard my heart and my mind. I now realize that it is my responsibility to take every thought captive to the obedience of Christ. I choose to believe the truth and I reject the lies of Satan. I will not pay attention to any thoughts that are contrary to what is true or lovely or right.

Forgive me for the times that I have ever doubted You. Forgive me for the times I paid attention to deceiving spirits. In the name of Christ, I resist the evil one, and I focus my mind on Jesus. You are the author and perfecter of my faith. Amen.

FALSE
PROPHETS

One late afternoon I was sitting in a coffee shop waiting for my son to finish soccer practice. A young man noticed I was reading my Bible and asked if I was studying to be a Christian. I told him I'd been a Christian for some time, and I asked him if he had ever made a decision for Christ. He said he had just become a Christian.

He told me that two friends had given a prophecy for him specifying what he should do with his life. He was troubled because the prophecies were not the same. "Which one should I believe?" he asked. "Neither one," I suggested. I asked him if he believed in the priesthood of believers. He said he wasn't sure, so I explained to him that all of God's children have access to Him. I asked him, "If God wanted you to do something, wouldn't He tell you?"

Understanding the gift of prophecy and distinguishing it from the role of a prophet may be the biggest battle for the church at the end of the twentieth century.[1] Certainly we don't want to limit the Lord from speaking to the church and His followers in these critical days. But if we don't ask hard questions and aren't open to other viewpoints, we may do just that or, even worse, end up paying attention to a false prophet. How can we tell the difference between the counterfeit and the real?

Differences of Opinion

At one extreme we have Christians who believe that the miraculous presence of God is no longer evident, that God speaks to His church only through the written Word of God as understood by elite theologians or pastors. They would deny that latter sentiment, but if you disagree with them, it comes through loud and clear that their faith is grounded in their perception and theological persuasion. These believers can be identified by their demand for loyalty and their need to be right as opposed to a sense of security in Christ and the need to be loving.

At the other end of the spectrum are Christians who deliberately try to get God to manifest Himself in every public worship. Their goal is to enter into the "holy of holies" and have prophecies, words of knowledge, healings, tongues and every other manifestation hinted at or eluded to in the Bible present every time they assemble.

The first group sits outside the spiritual world and critiques it. They don't worship God—they evaluate the worship service. They are more concerned about platform procedure than divine presence. The second group enters into the spiritual world, but nobody is critiquing! It is "holy" abandonment.

Where is the balance between dead orthodoxy and zeal without knowledge? While I can't draw an absolute line between these matters, I think we can agree on some broad concepts from the warnings of Scripture. Let's start by taking a look at biblical history.

The Need for Prophets

God created mankind to rule over the birds of the sky, the beasts of the fields and the fish of the sea. His dominion extended over the earth, its atmosphere and oceans. When Adam sinned, he lost his relationship with God and forfeited his rule over creation. Satan became the rebel holder of authority and is now the prince of the power of the air and the ruler of this world. God's redemptive plan is to defeat the god of this world and restore a fallen humanity, establishing His kingdom so the will of God will be done on earth as it is in heaven.

The Bible reveals God's plan. It includes historical accounts of the progress of His unfolding plan, the establishment and commissioning of the church, and the assurance that His eschatological plan for the future will be accomplished. Where we stand presently and how God has communicated to us is summarized in Ephesians 2:19-22:

> So then you are no longer strangers and aliens, but you are fellow citizens with the saints, and are of God's household, having been built upon the foundation of the apostles and prophets, Christ Jesus Himself being the corner stone, in whom the whole building, being fitted together is growing into a holy temple in the Lord; in whom you also are being built together into a dwelling of God in the Spirit.

God has delivered us from the domain of darkness and transferred us to the kingdom of His Son (Colossians 1:13). We are no longer sinners, but saints who sin. We are securely in God's household, seated with Christ in the heavenlies. Based on the foundation that has been laid by the apostles and prophets, we are being built up into a holy temple. The church has been established as a dwelling of God in the Spirit.

The means by which God has communicated this redemptive plan of His so clearly revealed in the Bible is through the prophets and the apostles. In addition, the ultimate revelation of God was Jesus Himself, the cornerstone of the church.

So Old Testament prophets were messengers of God. They never spoke presumptuously. God said to Moses, "Now then go, and I, even I, will be with your mouth, and teach you what you are to say" (Exodus 4:12); "I will raise up a prophet from among their countrymen like you, and I will put My words in his mouth, and he shall speak to them all that I command him" (Deuteronomy 18:18). God said to Jeremiah, "Behold, I have put My words in your mouth" (Jeremiah 1:9). And Ezekiel received this instruction: "But you shall speak My words to them whether they listen or not, for they are rebellious" (Ezekiel 2:7).

When Old Testament prophets spoke, it was "Thus saith the Lord." They spoke with authority because it was God's message, not man's. The test of a true prophet was that he was never wrong (Deuteronomy 18:20-22). People needed to discern whether a prophet was a true or false prophet, but they were not left with the responsibility of deciding what part of a prophecy was right and what part was wrong. If any part was wrong, the man was a false prophet. Unfortunately, they listened to a lot of false prophets and stoned a lot of true prophets because they didn't want to hear what the true prophets had to say. The Old Testament is one account after another of rebellious kings, Baal worship and false prophets.

Old Testament history closes with a 400-year silence during which the world was without a prophetic voice. Then the Word became flesh and dwelt among us (John 1:14). God was about to speak again, but it's interesting to note that even Jesus didn't speak on His own initiative: "For I did not speak on My own initiative, but the Father Himself who sent Me has given Me commandment, what to say, and what to speak" (John 12:49). Then after a year of public ministry, Jesus appointed twelve disciples who were identified as apostles after Pentecost. They carried God's message in the early days of the church.

Does God Use Prophets Today?

Most biblical scholars believe there are no longer any prophets and apostles who speak with the absolute authority of "Thus saith the Lord." Yet one cannot exclude the possibility that God could send someone to function as a prophet or apostle again.

Some have suggested that there are two prophets in Revelation 11:3, but the passage says they are "witnesses" who prophesy. What's the difference? They are identified as witnesses, but what they *do* is prophecy. In a similar fashion, some would call me a seminary professor who exhorts. A seminary professor is a person; exhortation is a gift. The first describes my position, the latter my gift.

Regarding today's prophets, are we to accept what they say as authoritative for the church in the same way we understand Scripture to be? Since the church pronounced that the canon of Scripture has been closed, many false teachers and false prophets, such as Joseph Smith (founder of the Mormons), have arisen claiming new revelation beyond the Scriptures. Islam claims divine revelation in addition to the Bible, and yet the message of the Koran is in conflict with the prophets and the apostles of the Bible. The same is true of the message of the Mormon Church.

One cannot say with absolute authority that God can't add to His Word, although we are clearly warned not to do so. Scripture teaches that the foundation has already been laid (past tense) by the apostles and prophets. God's plan has already been declared, we have been commissioned, and the future has been assured.

Yet God is still working today as He has in the past, through people. Prophets like Isaiah and apostles like Paul were people. The church has gifted people, and the gift of prophecy functions like other gifts within the church. But the New Testament gift of prophecy is not the same as the Old Testament office of prophet. If you have the gift of administration you are enabled by God to help structure the church and organize its efforts, but you probably will not be known only as an administrator. If you have the gift of exhortation, do people identify you as the exhorter? You may have the gift of tongues, but I'm fairly safe in saying that nobody refers to you as the tongue! Neither does the gift of prophecy necessarily make you a prophet. We are all simply children of God, supernaturally gifted to help build up one another to live righteous lives.

God builds upon the foundation that has already been laid by the apostles and prophets by giving us evangelists and pastor/teachers (Ephesians 4:11,12). Evangelists and pastor/teachers are people ordained by God to equip the saints so they (the saints) may reach their communities for Christ and build up one another.

Although Satan is defeated, the kingdom of darkness is still present in the church age. Along with the true evangelists, pastors, teachers and others gifted by God for ministry, expect Satan to have his false prophets, teachers and messiahs. Such is the case, and we have been warned sufficiently in the Scriptures. So let's examine how to identify false prophets and teachers, first from the Old Testament and then from the New Testament.

Identifying Old Testament False Prophets

The standard way of identifying an Old Testament prophet has already been mentioned. Deuteronomy 18:20-22 explains that if an alleged prophet spoke presumptuously (i.e., his own thoughts, not God's), the prophet was to die. If what he said didn't come true, he was a false prophet. That test works only when the words of the prophet predict some future event. As we shall see shortly, that wasn't the primary function of a true prophet.

Deuteronomy 13:1-3 identifies an even more insidious nature of false prophets to be discerned:

> If a prophet or a dreamer of dreams arises among you and gives you a sign or a wonder, and the sign or the wonder comes true, concerning which he spoke to you, saying, "Let us go after other gods (whom you have not known) and let us serve them," you shall not listen to the words of that prophet or that dreamer of dreams; for the Lord your God is testing you to find out if you love the Lord your God with all your heart and with all your soul.

In this case the signs and wonders come true, but their purpose is to lead people away from God to serve other gods. These dreamers of dreams are rebellious at heart (Deuteronomy 13:5). They use signs and wonders to lure people off the true path, and a gullible public follows blindly because they accept anything supernatural as being from God. The purpose is to get people dependent upon miraculous interventions, instead of the Word of God, as the means to know God's will. In Old Testament times God considered their evil so great that He required their life by the hands of their own family members (Deuteronomy 13:4-10).

Several years ago I had a college ministry near Long Beach, California. A nearby ministry created quite a controversy. Everybody was hearing about the great signs and wonders coming true at the hands of its young prophet. Several students under my ministry went to the Friday evening services which were held in a rented theater. God seemed to be blessing that work far more than mine. Eventually, though, the "prophet" moved his ministry and a few years later he died of AIDS as a result of his decadent lifestyle. A lot of people were led down the wrong path.

How can we identify a false prophet like that? Jeremiah 23:21-32 contains the most extensive discussion on this in the Old Testament:

> I did not send these prophets, but they ran. I did not speak to them, but they prophesied. But if they had stood in My council, then they would have announced My words to My people, and would have turned them back from their evil way and from the evil of their deeds (verses 21,22).

Notice that there are two errors. They were doing evil deeds and they were going down the wrong path.

Prophets were only to announce God's words, and the primary purpose was to call people to turn away from sin. They called people back to the moral standards of the law. They were to declare the way of the Lord, exhorting people to turn from their evil ways and accept God's plan for their lives.

The false prophets Jeremiah speaks of have only dreams, and believing them to be from God, they prophesy in the name of the Lord (Jeremiah 23:25). If you have a dream that you believe is from God, then understand the relative value of dreams. Jeremiah 23:28-29 explains:

> "The prophet who has a dream may relate his dream, but let him who has My word speak My word in truth. What does straw have in common with grain?" declares the LORD. "Is not My word like fire?" declares the LORD, "and like a hammer which shatters a rock?"

Being an old farm boy, I know the relative value of straw. If you try to feed straw to cattle, they won't eat it because it has no nutritional value. It makes good bedding, but only grain has nutritional value. God says a dream is like straw, but His Word is like wheat, and we will only grow when we devour God's Word. When we substitute the chaff of dreams for the wheat of biblical truth, we will soon become spiritually starved.

God is also against prophets who "steal [His] words from each other" (Jeremiah 23:30). Notice they are God's words, but false prophets have stolen them from others, and share them as though God has given the words to them. That's called plagiarism.

In addition, God is against prophets "who use their tongues and declare, 'The Lord declares' " (Jeremiah 23:31). This is subtly happening in our churches. I had a pulpit committee stop by my office for advice. The grandson of a former pastor had called the church and told them that God had revealed to him he was to be the new pastor. They were split as a committee.

Some reasoned that if God had spoken to this man, they'd better obey God and extend him an invitation. I asked what the young man was like. They said he seemed legitimate, but they were troubled by his request for absolute authority to carry out the plan God had given him.

I asked, "Don't you think God will work through the group that is responsible?" In this case it was the pulpit committee. I wanted to suggest that stones may be the best response to this young "prophet"! If God burdened my heart to pastor a congregation, I would wait for the call from the people responsible. If God hasn't burdened their hearts the same way, I would understand my desire to be from the flesh or the pit rather than from God.

A more subtle form of this is name dropping. Like the lovesick man who says to his date, "I have prayed about it, and God has revealed to me that we should get married." The man who asks for my daughter's hand had better come with a proposal, not a mandate. My wife calls this "pulling spiritual rank." Those who use God's name to get leverage for what they want can only expect disaster down the road. God says He's against the prophet who pulls spiritual rank by using His name to achieve personal objectives.

Finally God says, "I am against those who have prophesied false dreams and related them, and led My people astray by their falsehoods and reckless boasting" (Jeremiah 23:32). I'm troubled by those who have to keep promising great things in order to keep the money coming in. "God is going to do a great work, a mighty work," or worse, "a new thing," they proclaim. None of these people is a candidate for the Nobel Peace Prize, but Mother Theresa received one. Reckless boasting is not of God.

Identifying New Testament False Prophets and Teachers

The gift of prophecy in the New Testament has the same purpose of turning people's hearts back to God as did the Old Testament prophets. According to 1 Corinthians 14:24,25:

> But if all prophesy, and an unbeliever or an ungifted man enters, he is convicted by all, he is called to account by all; the secrets of his heart are disclosed; and so he will fall on his face and worship God, declaring that God is certainly among you.

God's Word is like fire; it purifies the church: "For it is time for judgment to begin with the household of God" (1 Peter 4:17). God is far more concerned about church purity than church growth. Because only the pure church can grow and bear fruit, Satan will use signs and wonders to lead people off the path of righteousness. He will deceive people to become obsessed with physical healings and external phenomena instead of heart purification. God's Word is like a hammer that breaks up the hard ground and softens the heart. If people were living in immorality in our churches and a word of prophecy came from the Lord, rest assured it would not be some generic source of comfort but an exhortation to purify ourselves.

The warnings against false prophets are numerous in the New Testament:

> Beloved, do not believe every spirit, but test the spirits to see whether they are from God; because many false prophets have gone out into the world (1 John 4:1).

The warnings intensify as the Lord prepares to return. In the Olivet discourse, Jesus said:

> And many false prophets will arise, and will mislead many. . . . For false Christs and false prophets will arise and will show great signs and wonders, so as to mislead, if possible, even the elect (Matthew 24:11,24).

Knowing that they will appear is one thing, but detecting who they are is another.

In determining the credibility of a prophet, the first thing I would look for is a *righteous life*. Jesus said, "You will know them by their fruits" (Matthew 7:20). The next three verses identify the counterfeits. They may say, "Lord, Lord!" They may prophesy, cast out demons and even perform miracles in the name of the Lord. Yet they will not enter the kingdom of heaven because they are not doing the will of the Father in heaven. Satan is obviously able to pull off miracles and get his demons to cooperate by leaving those they afflict at the right time. Thus it would appear that the false teacher had cast out demons. Jesus is not into "show time" and declares, "He who does the will of God will enter heaven."

It isn't what we do for God externally that gets us into heaven. It's what God has done for us internally. God's will for our life is our sanctification (1 Thessalonians 4:3). God has changed our nature; we must change our behavior. We are to be holy for He is holy (1 Peter 1:16). There will be those who will show great signs and wonders, but they will also hear from God, "Depart from Me you who practiced lawlessness" (Matthew 7:23). The false teachers hide their sin, but eventually their deeds will find them out. Paul reveals in 2 Corinthians 11:13-15:

> For such men are false apostles, deceitful workers, disguising themselves as apostles of Christ. And no wonder, for even Satan disguises himself as an angel of light. Therefore it is not surprising if his servants also disguise themselves as servants of righteousness; whose end shall be according to their deeds.

Eventually, the immorality of their lifestyle will be revealed.

The above passage reveals a second characteristic of false prophets and teachers. *They work within the church.* These are not cult leaders. Cults can be identified by their doctrine, and they make no attempt to hide it. Not so with false prophets and teachers:

> But false prophets also arose among the people, just as there will also be false teachers among you, who will secretly introduce destructive heresies, even denying the Master who bought them, bringing swift destruction upon themselves. And many will follow their sensuality, and because of them the way of the truth will be maligned; and in their greed they will exploit you with false words; their judgment from long ago is not idle, and their destruction is not asleep (2 Peter 2:1-3).

False teachers work secretly and under disguise as ministers of righteousness. What we *see* will seldom threaten the church. External opposition has had a purging effect on the church that usually leaves the church stronger. But these false teachers are infiltrators. Many are hard-core Satanists trained to infiltrate the church. Their purpose is to secretly introduce destructive heresies. Heretics are people who cause schisms. Heresy seldom begins with blatant error. It usually begins with truth out of balance. They will set us up with enough truth to choke us on subtle deviations. They may lure people by their dynamic personalities, causing people to follow their sensuality. The result is that many people will be mesmerized and follow their destructive ways.

A third characteristic of false prophets and teachers is their *rebellious heart.* They despise authority (2 Peter 2:10). If they are not in a leadership position, they will seek to discredit legitimate Christian leaders. This may be the easiest way to spot them. They won't answer to anyone. They have an independent spirit and not a compatible spirit with those desiring to do God's will. True Christian leaders have a servant's heart. True leaders don't seek to lord it over others, but prove to be an example.

Cautions Are in Order

As you guard against false prophets, I caution you not to go on a witch hunt. Many heresy hunters are self-righteous and as bad as the heretics they find. They become experts on what's wrong as opposed to what's right. Remember that good people can be deceived. If you come across someone who is a victim of bad teaching, show him the light—not the exit. The best way to eliminate the darkness is to turn on the light. Be a proclaimer, not a denouncer. And commit yourself to the truth. Fellowship in a place where truth is proclaimed in a balanced way.

Care is also needed in the area of judging morality. Don't throw somebody out because of one moral indiscretion. The issue is "those who practice lawlessness." Even then be careful, because there are many who have accepted God's standards and seem to desire to live a righteous life, but for some reason they cannot. They aren't false teachers because they aren't trying to teach anybody. Our hearts need to go out to such people because they are enslaved to sinful habits or are being blinded and held captive by Satan.

The Gift of Prophecy

I'm concerned about the growing misuse of the gifts of prophecy and words of knowledge. Perspective is the value of distance. Step back from the details of 1 Corinthians 12—14, the classic passage on spiritual gifts. What is Paul trying to say? There are a variety of spiritual gifts and manifestations of the Spirit. In the midst of this diversity, there is unity, because there is only one Spirit and one Lord. God gives the gifts as He wills. Gifts and manifestations come and go and come again for the purpose of accomplishing God's will. What remains is faith, hope and love. These are the lasting and continuous standards by which we evaluate our ministry and lives.

Paul says, "I write so that you may know how one ought to conduct himself in the household of God, which is the church of the living God, the pillar and support of the truth" (1 Timothy 3:15). Truth is the object of our faith. If we know the truth, it will set us free to grow in love with the hope of eternity before us. The church is gifted to accomplish that objective. Gifts are only a means to an end, never an end in themselves. When "gifts" become an end in themselves they are counterfeit, or else they become the basis for spiritual pride. Godly character is our goal, and it must take precedence over the gifts.

In 1 Corinthians 14, Paul is specifying the proper use of the gifts of prophecy and tongues in public worship. Some have understood verse 1 to be teaching that we are to earnestly desire the gift of prophecy. I understand the passage to teach that we are to desire the gift of prophecy over the gift of tongues in public worship. The congregation can only be edified by that which they can comprehend with their minds, therefore the elevation of prophecy over tongues. Tongues were not even to be used in public worship unless there was an interpretation.

The overwhelming thrust of the rest of Scripture encourages us to seek God and trust Him to gift us as He sees fit for the edification of the church. "Seek not, forsake not" seems to be the balance we need. Our responsibility is to yield to the Holy Spirit. However He chooses to fill us is His responsibility.

The Misuse of Prophecy

The Bible says there is only one intermediary between God and man, and that is Jesus. When God does send a prophet like Nathan to someone like David, for example, it is for the purpose of bringing conviction in order to establish righteousness. In the church age, bringing conviction is a primary ministry of the Holy Spirit.

The proper use of the gift of prophecy would reveal unrighteousness in order to establish people in Christ. Once people are living righteously with the Lord, the Holy Spirit will lead them. False gifts will not consistently promote holiness but will specify decisions concerning direction in life. That function is the role of the Holy Spirit alone: "For all those being led by the Spirit of God, these are the sons of God" (Romans 8:14).

Too many churches encourage their members, including the immature, to come into the fullness of the Spirit with manifestations. I ask, "Why not the fullness of the truth?" It's the fullness of the truth the Holy Spirit has promised to lead us into. I'm deeply concerned for young converts in ministries that push for them to seek total manifestations of the Spirit. Many have not had the time to understand the foundation laid by the apostles and the prophets. The church at Corinth had similar problems. They were exhorted by Paul to get back to the basics of faith, hope and love, and govern very closely the use of tongues and prophecies in public worship because God does everything decently and in order (1 Corinthians 14:40).

A pastor friend of mine received a letter from a former staff member who was also pastoring a church in his community. The letter contained a prophecy for my friend's church. I asked, "Why would God give a prophecy for your church through the pastor of another church?" I suggested that they shouldn't listen to it since it would function like a curse. From the time they heard it, everything that happened in the church would be evaluated by the prophecy (either to substantiate or invalidate it). They called the pastor of an exceptionally good charismatic church who advised them in the same way. If a person or church is earnestly seeking the Lord, God will work through the lines of authority that He has established in His Word.

Paul says, "Examine everything carefully; hold fast to that which is good" (1 Thessalonians 5:19-21).

Keeping Your Faith in Balance

If you accept prophetic utterances as valid for today, I would encourage you to test them in the following ways.

First, is the person giving the prophetic utterance living a balanced and righteous lifestyle?

Second, is the person committed to building God's kingdom or his own; is Christ being lifted up or is he?

Third, does the prophetic utterance establish confidence in the Word of God and is it consistent with a balanced presentation of it? Are people going to have a greater dependency upon God's revelation or man's inspiration? Are prophetic utterances a substitute for the serious, personal study of God's Word?

Fourth, does the use of the spiritual gift bring unity to the church and build up one another? Be careful in this test, because those who hold to a form of godliness but deny its power are not in balance either. They will quench the Spirit through censorship and very little will be accomplished in the church. They can cause disunity as well.

Last, do the spiritual manifestations bypass the mind? God operates through our mind; Satan bypasses it. If a person takes on a medium-like trance, be assured it is occultic. God renews our mind and brings back to our mind all that He has taught us. We are to think so as to have sound judgment.

All of us receive input from a myriad of sources today. With Satan still using false prophets in his battle for our minds, will you join me in this prayer that we may discern the truth God wants us to know to set and keep us free?

Dear Heavenly Father, I desire above all else to know Your will. I long for Your presence to be known in my life and ministry. I seek to glorify You by bearing much fruit.

But dear Lord, I don't want to possess any counterfeit gifts or follow any false teachers or prophets. Every spiritual manifestation in my life I bring before You. If it isn't of You, I renounce it and ask Your forgiveness for not being more discerning. If what I have experienced in my life is from You, then I pray that You would enable me to use it for Your glory. I will have only one Lord in my life, and that is You, Heavenly Father.

I commit myself to maturing in love and to meeting the needs of those around me. I choose to develop my faith by the truth of Your Word. I wish not to be identified with a wicked and adulterous generation that seeks only after a sign. You have already proven Your love for me by sending Your Son to die in my place. I love You and ask again for You to fill me with Your Holy Spirit that I may be holy as You are holy. Amen.

FACING FEAR

A fter speaking at a pastor's breakfast, I was swapping stories with several former students. We were sharing our experiences of helping people find freedom. One pastor, who was a stranger to the rest of us, was taking it all in. Seizing the right opportunity, he commented, "This is really interesting. Tell me, what would you do with the lady I'm seeing this afternoon? She's having terrible nightmares, she hears voices in her head and she has a lot of fear. That's just neurosis, isn't it?"

"What's she afraid of?" I responded. "She appears to have the classic symptoms of spiritual conflict. With cooperation, it usually takes less than two hours to free a person from that kind of attack."

I responded that way because in helping people resolve their spiritual conflicts, I have yet to see one who wasn't struggling with fear. How can we walk with God if fear is running our lives?

Fear is a powerful controller. It either compels us to do what is irresponsible or it impedes us from living responsibly. Recently a denominational executive spoke in our chapel and his opening statement was, "As I travel among our pastors, I'm overwhelmed by the realization that the number-one motivation in their life is fear of failure."

After several years of teaching evangelism and overseeing evangelistic outreaches, I can tell you with confidence that the number-one reason people don't share their faith is fear. Agoraphobia, fear of being in public, is one of the fastest growing psychological disorders. Fear of failure, fear of the devil, fear of man, fear of everything is plaguing our society.

Did you know that the most frequent command of Jesus in the Gospels is, "Fear not"? In anticipation of the entrance into the promised land, God tells His people four times, "Be strong and courageous" (see Joshua 1). The writer of Proverbs says, "The wicked flee when no one is pursuing, but the righteous are as bold as a lion" (Proverbs 28:1). It is characteristic of the Spirit-filled life to be bold:

> And when they had prayed, the place where they had gathered together was shaken, and they were all filled with the Holy Spirit, and began to speak the word of God with boldness (Acts 4:31).

The early church didn't pray for "divine appointments"; they prayed for boldness. God's kingdom can only be established by faithful and courageous people.

The fact that God doesn't look favorably on cowards and unbelievers is made evident in Revelation 21:7,8:

> He who overcomes shall inherit these things, and I will be his God and he will be My son. But for the cowardly and unbelieving and abominable and murderers and immoral persons and sorcerers and idolaters and all liars, their part will be in the lake that burns with fire and brimstone, which is the second death.

Does it surprise you that cowardly, unbelieving people were listed in a rogue's gallery with murderers and liars?

Why We Fear What We Fear

Fear and anxiety are similar, but not exactly the same. People are anxious because they don't know what is going to happen and they concern themselves with the worst. Fear, on the other hand, has an object. People fear *something*.

In order for a fear object to be legitimate, it must have two attributes. First, it has to be potent. Second, it has to be imminent. We fear that which threatens our well-being, but only when it's present.

For instance, I have a healthy fear of rattlesnakes. But as I'm writing this, I am not afraid. Why? Because there are no rattlesnakes present. If someone dropped by my office and threw one of those babies at my feet, you would see an immediate fear response. The snake is now both present and potent. But if you threw a dead snake into my office, I again would not be afraid once I made sure it was dead! The snake is present, but it's not potent. You can overcome fear by eliminating one (or both) of the attributes of the fear object.

Fear objects range from the inanimate and abstract (abandonment, heights, failure, fire) to the personal and real (parents, boss, God, Satan). Fears are learned. For example, a child learns a healthy fear of fire by getting burned. Unless the lesson is extreme or abusive, such development is good for self-preservation. But some early learning may not reflect reality. For instance, a little child may be warned not to go outside because the bogeyman is there. That child grows into an adult who fears leaving the house at night. Learned fears are not always rational and may result in phobias.

Phobias are irrational fears that don't reflect present-day reality. In early childhood, my wife witnessed a major airplane crash. Years later she lost a loved one in another airplane disaster. Her processing of those tragedies left her with a fear of flying. While it's a fact that airplane travel is far safer than automobiles, such reasoning may not resolve my wife's problem. Her fear is triggered in the present, but it was developed in the past.

Whether the original fear object was real or imagined doesn't affect the present emotional response. To the person experiencing fear, the fear is real.

There is a trilogy of fear objects which frighten almost everyone. Yet Scripture tells us we don't have to fear them. If we can conquer our fear of these three things, we will set ourselves free from the crippling fear Satan uses to destroy our walk with God. We'll take a look at these fear objects and examine what God has to say about them.

People Who Intimidate

The first major fear object is *man*. Consider Psalm 118:5-9:

> From my distress I called upon the Lord; The Lord answered me and set me in a large place. The Lord is for me; I will not fear; What can man do to me? The Lord is for me among those who help me; Therefore I shall look with satisfaction on those who hate me. It is better to take refuge in the Lord than to trust in man. It is better to take refuge in the Lord than to trust in princes.

The timid man is quick to respond, "What can man do to me? I'll tell you what man can do to me. He can abuse me, he can fire me from my job, he can even kill me."

True, but Jesus tells us to lay those fears aside: "And do not fear those who kill the body, but are unable to kill the soul; but rather fear Him who is able to destroy both soul and body in hell" (Matthew 10:28). If you fail to take God as your refuge, the fear of man will control your life.

God appointed Saul to be the first king of Israel and commanded him to utterly destroy Amalek along with all of his family, followers and possessions. Unfortunately, Saul didn't listen:

> But Saul and the people spared Agag and the best of the sheep, the oxen, the fatlings, the lambs, and all that was good, and were not willing to destroy them utterly; but everything despised and worthless, that they utterly destroyed (1 Samuel 15:9).

Then God said, "I regret that I have made Saul king, for he has turned back from following Me, and has not carried out My commands" (1 Samuel 15:11). Samuel confronted Saul, and after Saul's excuses ran out, he confessed, "I have sinned; I have indeed transgressed the command of the Lord and your words, because I feared the people and listened to their voice" (1 Samuel 15:24). Then the Lord rejected Saul as king of Israel. More than one king has gone down the tubes for fearing man more than God.

Suppose a secretary is intimidated by her boss. She works in fear of him from eight to five because he is both imminent and potent. What power does the boss have over the secretary? He could fire her! How could she overcome that power? She could quit or be willing to quit. By not allowing her boss to hold the job over her head, she would free herself from his intimidations.

I'm not suggesting that she rebel against her boss or become irresponsible. Servants are to obey their master and we are to work heartily as for the Lord rather than men (Colossians 3:22,23). However, when the secretary makes God her sanctuary, she frees herself up to live a responsible life. If she loses her job in the process, she has the assurance that God will meet all her needs.

Disarming the Fear of People

The means by which we overcome people's intimidations is to sanctify Christ as the Lord of our lives. When we make God our refuge, other fear objects pale in comparison. Look at 1 Peter 3:13-15:

> And who is there to harm you if you prove zealous for what is good? But even if you should suffer for the sake of righteousness, you are blessed. And do not fear their intimidation, and do not be troubled, but sanctify Christ as Lord in your hearts, always being ready to make a defense to every one who asks you to give an account for the hope that is in you, yet with gentleness and reverence.

It's important to note when standing up to intimidating people that we are not to become like them in their belligerence. Our response in Christ is to give evidence of the fruit of the Spirit. We are to speak in gentleness and reverence.

Peter continues, "And keep a good conscience so that in the thing in which you are slandered, those who revile your good behavior in Christ may be put to shame" (1 Peter 3:16). As long as we abide in Christ and respond in grace, be assured that the other person's character will reveal itself. Let your intimidator bear the shame if anyone must.

Learning how to respond to the intimidations of people is essential to overcoming the first fear in the fear trilogy—man.

The Fear of Dying

The second member of the fearful trilogy is *death*. Most phobias can be reduced to a fear of death. It looms over many as the ultimate fear object. The fact that death is imminent is clearly established in Scripture: "It is appointed for men to die once, and after this comes the judgment" (Hebrews 9:27).

But Christians need not fear death. Jesus removed death as a legitimate fear object by taking away its power when He died for our sins: "Death is swallowed up in victory. O death, where is your victory? O death, where is your sting?" (1 Corinthians 15:54,55) Jesus Himself said, "I am the resurrection and the life. He who believes in Me shall live even if he dies. And everyone who lives, and believes in Me shall never die" (John 11:25,26).

Every child of God is spiritually alive, and even physical death cannot separate us from the love of God (Romans 8:38). Paul says, "For to me, to live is Christ, and to die is gain" (Philippians 1:21). Why? Because we have made God our sanctuary. When we physically die, we will receive a resurrected body and be far better off than we are today. Try putting something else into Paul's formula, for instance: "For me to live is success." Then to die would be what? Loss! "For me to live is a good physical body." Again, to die would be loss.

I often ask people, "What is the worst thing that could happen to you?" "Well, I could die," they answer. To which I respond, "Then you have nothing to fear, since the Bible says that may be the best thing that could happen to you!" The ultimate value is not physical life, but spiritual life. If our life is hid in Christ, then we won't suffer loss when we physically die. We can only gain. The person who is free from the fear of death is free to live today.

The Fear of Satan

The third member of the phobia trilogy is *Satan*. Fear is one of Satan's greatest strategies. We are cautioned in 1 Peter 5:8, "Be of sober spirit, be on the alert. Your adversary, the devil, prowls about like a roaring lion, seeking someone to devour." Lions roar in order to paralyze their prey in fear so they can consume them. I'm often asked, "Aren't you afraid to deal with demonic issues?"

I respond, "I don't know of one verse in the Bible that instructs us to fear Satan." Satan is a defeated foe, but through deception he paralyzes the church in fear.

In *The Bondage Breaker* I give the following illustration. When I was a young boy on the farm, our neighbors had a yappy little dog that scared the socks off me. I recall one day when my brother, father and I drove over to their farm. As soon as we got out of the pick-up, that dog came roaring around the corner barking like crazy. Terrorized, I ran! Guess who the dog chased? I found sanctuary on top of the pick-up. My brother and father stood right by the dog who was barking only at me. The dog didn't chase or bother them one bit. What power did that dog have to put me on top of that pick-up?

It had no inherent power at all. It was a puny little runt! The only power which it had was the power I gave to it. I'll tell you how I ended up on top of the truck. That dog used my mind, my will, my emotions and my muscles. My dad thought it was a little embarrassing. He wanted me to stand my ground. The next time we went to that farm, I worked up my courage and when the dog came after me I kicked a rock at it. To my great relief, it put its tail between its legs and took off.

James 4:7 offers this strategy: "Submit therefore to God. Resist the devil and he will flee from you." The order is critical. Make God your sanctuary first, then the devil can easily be resisted.

Another of Satan's tactics is the common psychological disorder, anxiety attacks. They're called anxiety rather than fear attacks because people don't know what they're afraid of. In my experience, when people can't identify the fear object, I can almost assure you it's Satan.

Because of the nature of my ministry, I've had several such attacks. I'm not by nature a timid person, but I have awakened at night terrorized. Knowing what it is, I know how to resolve it. Most people try to respond physically but can't. Anxiety attacks often feel like a pressure on the chest or something grabbing the throat. Since they can't respond physically, it seems as though the power is overwhelming. Responding in the flesh will not resolve it: "For the weapons of our warfare are not of the flesh, but are divinely powerful for the destruction of fortresses" (2 Corinthians 10:4).

Saying No to Satan

How then can we resist these attacks? Since Satan cannot touch who we are as children of God, inwardly we can always turn to God. The moment we turn to our authority and acknowledge Christ as the Lord of our life, we will be free to respond verbally. All we have to say is, "Jesus!" The need to say it cannot be overstated. Satan is under no obligation to obey our thoughts. We must take our stand verbally against that kind of attack. Notice the words in Matthew 10:25-27:

> It is enough for the disciple that he become as his teacher, and the slave as his master. If they have called the head of the house Beelzebub, how much more the members of his household! Therefore do not fear them, for there is nothing covered that will not be revealed, and hidden that will not be known. What I tell you in the darkness, speak in the light; and what you hear whispered in your ear, proclaim upon the housetops.

Why verbally? Because all occult practices are dark, mysterious and hidden. As soon as we expose them by bringing them to the light, their power is broken. God requires us to verbally take our stand in the world: "If you confess with your mouth Jesus as Lord, and believe in your heart that God raised him from the dead, you shall be saved" (Romans 10:9). People are intimidated by deceiving spirits. But as soon as the lie is exposed, the power of Satan is broken. I can illustrate this from my personal experience.

What would you do if a demonized person suddenly started to approach you? That's happened to me more than once in counseling. In one case, a rather large lady got out of her chair and started to come toward me. All I did was verbally say, "I'm a child of God. The evil one cannot touch me" (1 John 5:18). She stopped dead in her tracks.

A man on the east coast heard that account in a series of tapes that I had done. Shortly after that he was confronted by three thugs at a train station demanding his money. "It was as though I could see right through them," he told me later. So he responded, "I'm a child of God. The evil one can't touch me." "What?" they asked. He repeated, "I'm a child of God. The evil one can't touch me." "Oh!" they responded and walked away.

Satan can't do anything about our position in Christ. But if he can get us to believe it's not true, then we will live as though it's not, even though it is true. Knowing who we are as children of God cannot be overstated in making a stand against Satan. Notice the complete text of 1 John 5:18-20:

> We know that no one who is born of God sins; but He who was born of God keeps him and the evil one does not touch him. We know that we are of God, and the whole world lies in the power of the evil one. And we know that the Son of God has come, and has given us understanding, in order that we might know Him who is true, and we are in Him who is true, in His Son Jesus Christ. This is the true God and eternal life.

Acting Responsibly

Overcoming the fears of man, death and Satan is what frees us to live a responsible life. Irrational fears compel us to act irresponsibly, or they impede us from living a responsible life. In that sense fear and faith are mutually exclusive.

A severe storm was hitting the east coast, and the Coast Guard was summoned to respond to a ship in crisis. A young sailor, new on board, was terrorized by the prospect and proclaimed, "We can't go out. We'll never come back!" The seasoned captain responded, "We must go out. We don't have to come back." Duty called and responsibility overcame the fear.

If we're going to walk by faith, there can be only one fear object in our life, and that's God. We are responsible to Him. He is the ultimate fear object because He is omnipotent and omnipresent. The fear of the Lord is healthy because it is the one fear that expels all other fears. Notice how this is true from Isaiah 8:11-14:

> For thus the Lord spoke to me with mighty power and instructed me not to walk in the way of this people . . . and you are not to fear what they fear or be in dread of it. It is the Lord

of hosts whom you should regard as holy. And He shall be your fear, and He shall be your dread. Then He shall become a sanctuary.

All other fear objects pale in comparison to our holy God. We need to be like David who proclaimed before Goliath, "For who is this uncircumcised Philistine that he should taunt the armies of the living God?" (1 Samuel 17:26) The Hebrew army saw Goliath in relation to themselves and cowered in defeat. David saw Goliath in relation to God and conquered in His strength.

When the twelve spies checked out the promised land, ten of them came back and responded, "We are not able to go up against the people, for they are too strong for us" (Numbers 13:31). They didn't see God in the land, they saw the giants. So they reasoned, "We became like grasshoppers in our own sight, and so we were in their sight" (Numbers 13:33). (I saw myself as a grasshopper compared to that stupid dog I mentioned earlier, so I was a grasshopper in the dog's sight.) With that perspective, "all the congregation lifted up their voices and cried, and the people wept that night" (Numbers 14:1). (I felt like crying on top of that truck!) Joshua and Caleb responded:

> Only do not rebel against the Lord; and do not fear the people of the land, for they shall be our prey. Their protection has been removed from them, and the Lord is with us; do not fear them (Numbers 14:9).

The people did rebel. They accepted the majority report instead of listening to Caleb and Joshua. By accepting the Canaanites' will over God's will, they elevated the power and eminence of the Canaanites over the omnipotence and omnipresence of God. To honor God as the ultimate fear object is to worship Him. To be controlled by any other fear object is to allow it to usurp God's place in our lives.

Pleasing God

Obeying the commandment to have no other gods before us is the first act of worship. The writer of Proverbs says, "The fear of the Lord is the beginning of knowledge; fools despise wisdom and instruction" (Proverbs 1:7). To worship God is to acknowledge His divine attributes. He doesn't need us to tell Him who He is. We need to keep our minds renewed to the reality of His presence. The fear of God is the highest motivation to do good. Notice how this is brought out in 2 Corinthians 5:9-11:

> Therefore also we have as our ambition, whether at home or absent, to be pleasing to Him. For we must all appear before the judgment seat of Christ, that each one may be recompensed for his deeds in the body, according to what he has done, whether good or bad. Therefore knowing the fear of the Lord, we persuade men, but we are made manifest to God; and I hope that we are made manifest also in your consciences.

Realizing that God knows the thoughts and intentions of our hearts, we should be motivated to live our lives to please Him. Someday we're going to stand before Him and give an account. The judgment that Paul is talking about in this passage is not for punishment but for rewards. We don't fear God because of the possibility of punishment: "There is no fear in love, but perfect love casts out fear because fear involves punishment, and the one who fears is not perfected in love" (1 John 4:18). We have already been judged as to where we will spend eternity. But how we spend eternity depends on how we respond to God in this lifetime.

I personally don't want to limp into heaven and have Him say, "Well, okay, come on in." I want to stand before God someday and hear Him say, "Well done, good and faithful servant. Enter into the joy of your Lord." That's the greatest motivation in my life. As a child I didn't fear the spanking of my father nearly as much as the fear of disappointing my parents.

Resolving Your Fears

At the end of the chapter you will find a "Phobia Finder." I use it to help people identify and hopefully eliminate any irrational fears in their lives. Let's go through it and apply it to possible fear situations in our lives.

First, *analyze your fear*. Identify all fear objects. What is it you're afraid of? A problem well-stated is half solved. Most people aren't aware of what is controlling their lives. Remember,

"God has not given us a spirit of timidity, but of power, and love, and discipline" (2 Timothy 1:7).

If you are struggling with anxiety attacks, determine when they first occurred. What experience preceded the first attack? People struggling with agoraphobia can usually identify one precipitating event. It is often associated with some tragedy or failure in their lives. Satan takes advantage of victimized people if they don't seek a scriptural solution to their crisis. For example, I have found that affairs and abortions often precede anxiety attacks. When I established the connection, I discovered that the person had not resolved the sin before God. The person rationalized it instead of confessing it. The psalmist says, "For I confess my iniquity; I am full of anxiety because of my sin" (Psalm 38:18).

Second, *determine where God's place in your life has been usurped.* In what way does any fear prevent you from responsible behavior or compel you toward irresponsible behavior? You may need to confess any situations where you've allowed your actions to be controlled by fear. Remember, "The wicked flee when no one is pursuing, but the righteous are as bold as a lion" (Proverbs 28:1). We will always live less than a responsible life if we fear anything other than God. Sanctify Christ as the Lord of your life. Make God your sanctuary and commit yourself to live a responsible life according to His will.

Third, *work out a plan of responsible behavior.* A college student shared with me that she was living in terror of her father. They hadn't spoken to each other in six months. Obviously there was irresponsible behavior on both their parts. I asked her what she would be afraid of if she went home and assumed her role as her father's daughter. I suggested that she take the initiative that evening and say, "Hi, Dad!" We reasoned that there were three possible responses he could give. First, he could get mad. Second, he could respond with a greeting. Third, he could remain silent. It was the possibility of the third response that created the most fear.

We then discussed the fourth point in the Phobia Finder: *Determine in advance what your response will be to any fear object.* The young woman and I talked about what her response would be in each of those three cases we had mentioned. I then asked her if she would be willing to carry out our plan. She agreed to do it. I got a call that evening from a happy daughter who exclaimed, "He said 'Hi' back!"

Do the thing you fear the most, and the death of fear is certain. See what the Lord says in Psalm 91:1-5,9,10:

> He who dwells in the shelter of the Most High will abide in the shadow of the Almighty. I will say to the LORD, "My refuge and my fortress, my God, in whom I trust!" For it is He who delivers you from the snare of the trapper, and from the deadly pestilence. He will cover you with His pinions, and under His wings you may seek refuge; His faithfulness is a shield and bulwark. You will not be afraid of the terror by night, or of the arrow that flies by day; for you have made the LORD, my refuge, even the Most High, your dwelling place. No evil will befall you, nor will any plague come near your tent.

All of us have had the experience of being afraid, but how often have we stopped to realize how much fear can control our lives? Its paralysis can prevent us from knowing the direction, freedom and ministry God wants us to have. Join me in prayer, affirming God's dominion in our lives so that the power of fear is broken.

Dear Heavenly Father, You are the fortress, shield and strength of my life. I refuse to be intimidated by any fear object. I choose to sanctify Christ as the Lord of my life. You are the only omnipotent, omnipresent God. You have not given me a spirit of fear. By Your presence in my life I have power, love and a sound mind. Your power enables me to live a responsible life. Your presence in my life has made me a partaker of Your divine nature so I can love others as You love them. You are my sanctuary, and I ask You to protect my family and ministry. Amen.

Phobia Finder

1. Analyze your fear.
   a. Identify all fear objects. (What are you afraid of?)
   b. When did you first experience the fear (anxiety attack)?
   c. What events preceded the first occurrence?

2. Determine where God's place in your life has been usurped.
   a. In what way does any fear:

   Prevent you from responsible behavior?

   Compel you toward irresponsible behavior?
   b. Confess any active or passive participation on your part where you have allowed fear to control your life.
   c. Commit yourself to God with the understanding that you are willing to fulfill your responsibility in the matter.

3. Work out a plan of responsible behavior.

4. Determine in advance what your response will be to any fear object.

5. Commit yourself to carrying out the plan.

Part Two:

Divine Guidance

*Do you believe that the will of God
is good, acceptable and
perfect for you?*

6

THE ESSENTIAL PREREQUISITE

Knowing the will of God is not just a twentieth-century problem. People were struggling at the time of Christ. Some people were saying of Him, "He's a good man." Others were saying, "He leads the multitude astray" (see John 7:12). How could these people know whether He was leading them into truth?

Seizing the opportunity, Jesus set forth standards of divine guidance. His first admonition was, "My teaching is not mine, but His who sent me. If any man is willing to do His will, he shall know of His teaching, whether it is of God, or whether I speak from myself" (John 7:17). The essential prerequisite to knowing the will of God, according to Jesus, is a willingness to do it. Yet before we seek to understand why that is the case, let's ask an even more basic question: What is the will of God?

Understanding What God Wants

Notice the opening words of the Lord's Prayer:

Our Father Who art in heaven, hallowed be Thy name. Thy kingdom come. Thy will be done on earth as it is in heaven (Matthew 6:9,10).

When praying this prayer, we are asking for God's will to

71

be accomplished on earth as it presently is in heaven. Apparently God's will is being perfectly executed in heaven but not on earth. What has gone wrong on earth, and how is this to be understood in light of the coming of His kingdom? Let's step back to the beginning of time to understand the unfolding plan of God.

God created mankind in His own image. He breathed into them, and they became living beings. The first Adam was both spiritually and physically alive. He was physically alive in that his soul/spirit was in union with his body, and spiritually alive in that his soul/spirit was in union with God. Eve was created out of Adam and they were told to be fruitful and multiply. God charged them to rule over the birds of the sky, the beasts of the field and the fish of the sea. They were given dominion on earth over God's creation.

Then Satan approached Eve, tempting her in the same three ways we are tempted today: the lust of the flesh, the lust of the eyes and the boastful pride of life. Being deceived, she took the fruit and ate, and Adam followed likewise in sin. Because they acted independently of God through disobedience, they died spiritually and were separated from God. Satan became the rebel holder of authority—a position Jesus never questioned, calling him the "ruler of this world" (John 14:30).

Separated from God, Adam and Eve lived their lives independently of Him. Attempts at establishing an ongoing relationship through the government and law in the Old Testament would prove futile.

Like all offspring of Adam, we come into this world physically alive but spiritually dead. During the formative early years of our lives, we learn how to survive, cope, defend ourselves and hopefully succeed. We were conformed to this world because we had no other choice. We had neither the presence of God in our life nor the knowledge of His ways. Lacking a relationship with God, we sought to find our identity and purpose for living in the natural world. Paul expressed it this way:

> And you were dead in your trespasses and sins, in which you formerly walked according to the course of this world, according to the prince of the power of the air, of the spirit that is now working in the sons of disobedience. Among them we

too all formerly lived in the lusts of our flesh, indulging the desires of the flesh and of the mind, and were by nature children of wrath even as the rest (Ephesians 2:1-3).

How Jesus Fulfilled God's Plan

What a hopeless mess! If Jesus came to undo all of that, He had His work cut out for Him. Mankind was dead in trespasses and sin, and Satan was the ruler of the world. Nothing short of Jesus' death on the cross could undo both, so that is why He came. First John 3:8 says, "The Son of God appeared for this purpose, that He might destroy the works of the devil." Jesus said He came that we might have life (John 10:10). Was He successful? Look at Colossians 2:13-15:

> And when you were dead in your transgressions and the uncircumcision of your flesh, He made you alive together with Him, having forgiven us all our transgressions, having canceled out the certificate of debt consisting of decrees against us and which was hostile to us, and He has taken it out of the way, having nailed it to the cross. When he had disarmed the rulers and authorities, He made a public display of them, having triumphed over them through Him.

Jesus accomplished both tasks: He saved mankind and he disarmed Satan.

The Complete Gospel

First, let's take a look at what happened to mankind. If Jesus wanted to save a dead person He would have to do two things. He would first have to deal with what caused the dead man to die. In this case, "the wages of sin is death" (Romans 6:23). So He went to the cross and died for our sins. But that's only half the gospel.

We understand the fact that we are sinful and need a Messiah to die for our sins. So if we believe and trust in Jesus, our sins will be forgiven and when we die we will go to heaven. The greatest issue is that we were dead in our trespasses and sins and desperately needed life. The second thing Jesus did for mankind was that He gave us eternal life as a present reality and not just something we get when we die:

> And the witness is this, that God has given us eternal life, and this life is in His Son. He who has the Son has the life; he who does not have the Son of God does not have the life (1 John 5:11,12).

Every child of God is spiritually alive right now. Before we experienced salvation, we were conformed to this world and our minds were programmed to live independently of God. This learned independence is what constitutes the flesh. And though we have received eternal life, nobody pushed the "clear" button in our memory bank. We still have to deal with the flesh. That's why the apostle Paul writes in Romans 12:2:

> And do not be conformed to this world, but be transformed by the renewing of your mind, that you may prove what the will of God is, that which is good and acceptable and perfect.

God has given us eternal life but we must "work out our salvation with fear and trembling for it is God who is at work in us, both to will and to work for His good pleasure" (Philippians 2:12,13). Since our citizenship is in heaven, we need to prepare for that eternal state by living righteous lives. We are to become the children of God that our heavenly Father has called us to be.

The Lion Tamed

Jesus Christ has defeated Satan. Scripture assures us that Satan is a defeated foe, but according to 1 Peter 5:8 he roars around like a hungry lion seeking for someone to devour. He no longer has the teeth to do as he wishes, but he is gumming Christians to death! It is our responsibility to submit to God, resist the devil and he will flee from us (James 4:7). Jesus announced that "all authority has been given to Me in heaven and on earth" (Matthew 28:18). If we are going to go into the world and make disciples, we need to know that God has given us the authority to do His will. We should exercise authority over Satan when necessary.

Not only did Jesus complete that which He came to do (He said, "It is finished"), but He left us an example to follow in His steps (1 Peter 2:21). And what was His example? "My food is to do the will of Him who sent me, and to accomplish His work"

(John 4:34). Was it easy? Oh no! It may bring comfort to some that, in His humanity, Jesus struggled with the will of God. Jesus agonized in His darkest hour: "Father if Thou art willing, remove this cup from Me, yet not My will but Thine be done" (Luke 22:42). The Lord Jesus Christ modeled a life of total dependence upon God the Father.

Let me summarize God's will for our lives:

God's will for those who believe in Him is to be alive in Christ for the purpose of establishing His kingdom by overcoming the evil one and becoming fully the people He has called us to be.

The Heart of God's Will

In a personal sense, God's will for our lives is that we conform to the image of God, something the apostle Paul makes clear in 1 Thessalonians 4:3: "For this is the will of God, your sanctification." In his letter to Roman Christians, Paul writes, "For whom He foreknew He predestined to become conformed to the image of His son" (Romans 8:29) and adds in 1 Timothy 1:5, "The goal of our instruction is love from a pure heart, a good conscience, and a sincere faith."

I can hear the protests, "But that doesn't answer the questions you raised at the beginning of chapter 1." You're right. But divine guidance will never come to those whose primary goal is not first and foremost conforming to the image of God.

There is no instruction in the Bible concerning career choice, where we live or who we should marry. There is, however, an abundance of instruction on how we're to relate to our employer and behave on the job we already have (Colossians 3:22-25). And there is much about how to relate with one another (Colossians 3:10-14) and live with our families (Colossians 3:18-21).

The Bible overwhelmingly instructs that to do God's will means living in harmony with God and man:

> You shall love the Lord your God with all your heart, and with all your soul, and with all your mind. This is the great and foremost commandment. The second is like it, you shall love your neighbor as yourself. On these two commandments depend the whole law and the prophets (Matthew 22:37-40).

The whole purpose of the Bible is to teach us how to have a relationship with God and live in harmony with one another. We do this by assuming our responsibilities for today and trusting God for tomorrow.

Most people want to know what God has in store for them tomorrow. That's why prophecy has always been a popular subject. But most prophecy buffs know that the critical issue concerning the Lord's second coming is, "What sort of people ought you to be in holy conduct and godliness" (2 Peter 3:11). Jesus said, "But seek ye first His kingdom and His righteousness, and all these things shall be added to you, therefore do not be anxious for tomorrow" (Matthew 6:33,34). Biblical prophecy is given to us as a hope (the present assurance of some future good) so we will have the courage to live righteously and confidently today.

Again I can hear the protests, "Are you trying to tell us that we aren't to make any plans for the future or establish any goals for our ministry or work?" No, I'm trying to say that the primary focus of God's will is that we seek to establish His kingdom by becoming the person He wants us to be *today*. I'm not really sure that God's will enters into the choice of whether we become an engineer, plumber or nurse. But I am convinced that God's will is concerned with what kind of engineer, plumber or nurse we are.

I teach leadership and church management, so I believe in setting goals and making plans. But a biblical vision for the future and godly goals for ministry or work have no value if they don't provide direction for our steps today. Goals for tomorrow that don't prioritize present activities are nothing more than wishful thinking. We make plans for tomorrow in order to establish meaningful activities for today. We need to ask the Lord each day if we are still on target, and give Him the right to order mid-course changes in direction.

Making the Most of Every Opportunity

There are two important concepts about the will of God that my students hear at seminary. The first is, "Bloom where you are planted." Be the best you can be at your present assignment, and stay there until God calls you elsewhere.

Oftentimes my students will say, "There are no openings to serve at my church!" My response, "Oh, yes there are. They're probably begging for someone to teach third-grade boys." The momentary silence reveals this thought: "But anyone can teach third-grade boys. I had something bigger in mind." Like maybe an opening in the Trinity!

Take the opportunity before you and teach those third-grade boys. Decide to be the best teacher they've ever had. You may start with only three little boys, but at the end of that year you've got twelve boys excited about God, Sunday school and church. Next year, when the personnel committee needs to fill leadership positions, they say, "We need some new life on the Christian education committee." Somebody aware of the fruit you are bearing says, "There's this guy doing a bang-up job with our third graders. Let's ask him to be on the committee."

Now that you are on the Christian education committee, decide to be the best committee member you can be. It won't be long before they recognize your initiative and say, "We could use this person on the board." Determine to become the best possible board member you can. Then an opening develops for an intern and guess who the people suggest! People hearing of your faithfulness and aware of the fruit you are bearing ask you to consider a full-time pastoral position. So you become the best youth pastor, small group pastor or college minister you can possibly be. Before long you'll be bearing so much fruit that other churches will be inquiring about your availability. God guides those who bloom where they are planted.

When D. L. Moody found his life in Christ, he looked for some opportunities to teach at a church, but no one wanted to use the uneducated man. He started his own Bible study in a shoe store, and it wasn't long before kids were coming out of the woodwork. People couldn't help but notice him because he was bearing fruit, and few have left such an imprint as his upon the world.

Paul said, "I thank Christ Jesus our Lord, who has strengthened me, because He considered me faithful, putting me into service" (1 Timothy 1:12). Show yourself faithful by exploiting the opportunities around you. The needs of people are everywhere, so what are you waiting for?

What an elementary concept, but many simply bide their time waiting for the "big" opportunity. Sure, these people will humble themselves to teach third graders, but at the end of the year they have the same three boys they started with—boys who are now looking forward to being promoted out of their class. Jesus said to those who had bloomed where they were planted, "Well done, good and faithful servant; you were faithful with a few things, I will put you in charge of many things, enter into the joy of your master" (Matthew 25:21). If you aren't responsible in your present assignment and taking advantage of the opportunities that are there, don't expect God to call you elsewhere.

A man in my church often expressed his frustration with his job. For twenty years he'd been working as a construction worker, and he hated it! Frustrated with his career, he wondered why God wouldn't call him out of there.

I asked him if he had ever expressed dissatisfaction about his job with his fellow employees who weren't Christians. He said, "Oh, sure. I complain right along with the rest of them." I continued, "What do you suppose that does to your witness?" He was a little startled by my question. I added, "Do you realize that God has you exactly where He wants you? When you assume your responsibility to be the person God wants you to be as a construction worker, He may open a new door for you."

The Holy Spirit must have brought conviction because this man became a missionary at work. He displayed concern for the needs of his co-workers and their families and soon had a series of witnessing experiences to share. Within six months an opportunity arose and he left construction work. And all because he started to bloom where he was planted.

Moving in Obedience

The second important concept I teach about God's will is that God can only guide a moving ship. He is the rudder, but if the ship isn't under way it can't be directed. Willingness to obey His will gets the ship moving.

I was assigned to a destroyer when I was in the Navy. We had just passed through the Panama Canal on our way to San Diego when we had a flame-out in the middle of the night. The oil king (the man responsible for even distribution of the oil on board the ship) had allowed a compartment of oil to be pumped dry. In a short time the boilers went cold for lack of fuel, and we lost all our power. Within minutes our ship was doing 30- and 40-degree rolls. A ship without power is helpless in the sea. The helmsman could do nothing because the rudder only works if the ship is under way.

In Acts 15:36, Paul had decided to revisit the churches he helped establish on his first missionary trip. The churches were being strengthened and increasing in number (Acts 16:5). Luke reports:

> And they passed through the Phrygian and Galatian region, having been forbidden by the Holy Spirit to speak the word in Asia; and when they had come to Mysia, they were trying to go into Bithynia, and the Spirit of Jesus did not permit them; and passing by Mysia, they came down to Troas. And a vision appeared to Paul in the night: a certain man of Macedonia was standing and appealing to him, and saying, "Come over to Macedonia and help us" (Acts 16:6-9).

Sometimes God's leading does not make sense. If God wanted Paul to go to Macedonia in the first place, why didn't He make it easier and faster by having Paul travel by land to Caesarea and sail to Macedonia? Because God starts us out on a life course to fulfill a certain purpose and then, only when we are ready, He gives us course corrections. Like a good river pilot, He steers us away from troubled waters, and like a good coach, He never puts us in the game until we are ready.

If God wanted me to be a seminary professor, why didn't he direct me to a good Bible college and then immediately to seminary? Instead He allowed/guided me through a variety of experiences—farm boy, sailor, wrestling coach, aerospace engineer, campus pastor, youth pastor, minister of adult education and senior pastor. All the time I was gaining experience and developing character. Every new assignment was a stretching experience; each had a greater responsibility.

I believe in divine guidance. We read in Isaiah 58:11, "The Lord will continually guide you." But the context reveals that there are prerequisites that have to be satisfied. The Israelites were seeking God's leading through fasting (verse 2), but God revealed that their fasting was a farce which ended in strife (verse 4). The fast that God desired was proof of their repentance. He desired for them to set the captives free and meet the needs of the poor around them (verses 6,7). "Then your light will break out like the dawn" (verse 8). Then guidance would come.

Instead, the Israelites were like a person who seeks to be an athlete by simply suiting up for the race. That's not how the skills are gained. It's in the course of dedication, training and the contest itself that one gains the skill of an athlete.

It's in the doing of God's work that His will becomes known.

Abandonment to God's Will

I want to now return to the essential prerequisite that I mentioned at the beginning of the chapter, that in order to know God's will there must be a willingness to do it.

Imagine, if you would, a door in the path ahead of us. God's will is on the other side of that door. We crave to know what it is. Will God show us what's on the other side of that door? No. Why not? Because we have to resolve an issue on this side of the door first. If He is Lord, He has the right to determine what's on the other side of the door. If we don't afford Him that right, then we are not acknowledging Him as Lord.

Why do we want to know what's on the other side of that door? Isn't it because we want to reserve the right to determine whether or not we will go through it? Some boldly walk halfway through, but keep their foot in the door just in case they don't like what they see and want to go back. It's going to be awfully hard to continue walking with God if your foot is stuck in the door. Jesus said, "No one putting his hand to the plow and looking back is fit for the kingdom of God" (Luke 9:62).

One man probably spoke for many when he said, "I'm so used to running my own life. I'm not sure I even can or want to trust someone else. Besides, God would probably haul me off to some mission field I can't stand." What we need to realize is that if we did give our heart to the Lord, and God did call us to that mission field, by the time we got there we wouldn't want to be anywhere else.

Question: Do you believe that the will of God is good, acceptable and perfect for you? That's the heart of the issue. In the Lord's Prayer we are taught to approach God with the intent that His will be accomplished on earth. It makes no sense to petition God if we are not predisposed to do His will.

In the last half of the nineteenth century, George Mueller founded the Bristol Orphan Home which would become known all over the world as one of the most remarkable monuments of human faith and divine guidance in history. Year after year, without a single advertisement to the public or appeal to Christian friends, hundreds of children were fed, clothed and educated. The home was maintained simply through prayer and faith. George Mueller epitomizes the essential prerequisite to divine guidance in these thoughts:

> I seek in the beginning to get my heart in such a state that it has no will of its own in regard to a given matter. Nine-tenths of the trouble with people is just here. Nine-tenths of the difficulties are overcome when our hearts are ready to do the Lord's will. When one is truly in this state, it is usually but a little way to the knowledge of what His will is.

Knowing that "what's on the other side of the door" is something planned by our loving, omnipotent heavenly Father, would you pray this prayer with me?

Dear Heavenly Father, I choose to acknowledge You as the Lord of my life. Your loving kindness extends to all generations. You are the only all-powerful, all-knowing and ever-present Lord. I will have no other gods before me.

Forgive me for the times I have acted as my own god and sought to determine my own destiny. Forgive me for ever questioning that Your will for my life is anything but good, acceptable and perfect. I choose to no longer be conformed to this world, but to be transformed by the renewing of my mind.

I, therefore, commit myself to be a workman who needs not to be ashamed, rightly dividing the word of truth. By Your grace I determine to be faithful with what You have already entrusted me.

For this day, I commit myself to be the person You want me to be. I ask You to fill me with Your Holy Spirit and grant me the wisdom and guidance as I seek to do Your will. May Your kingdom rule extend to me. You are the king of my life. I submit to You. Amen.

*How do we give glory to another when
we are desperately looking
for affirmation ourselves?*

7

GLORIFYING
GOD

B y now your mind may be swirling with a lot of questions: "How do I know the will of God? What difference will it make if I discover the will of God, since I can't seem to run my life now? How can I ever please God with my rotten background?"

Let's examine some additional issues about knowing God's will, then we'll see how it impacts all of us, especially people who are hurting.

Heaven is where we say to God, "Thy will be done." Hell is where God says to us, "Thy will be done." As I said in the last chapter, the essential prerequisite to knowing the will of God is our disposition toward it. In dealing with the question of what is true and what isn't, who is right and who isn't, Jesus responds by saying, "If any man is willing to do His will, he shall know of the teaching, whether it is of God, or whether I speak of Myself" (John 7:17).

If we are predisposed to question or reject the will of God, we will never know what it is. Disobedience affects discernment. Getting my own way excludes God's way. God, speaking through the prophet Isaiah, says:

> For My thoughts are not your thoughts, nor are your ways My ways, declares the Lord. As the heavens are higher

than the earth, so are My ways higher than your ways, and My thoughts than your thoughts (Isaiah 55:8,9).

If I wanted to determine the spiritual vitality of an individual using only one criteria, I would evaluate whether the person desires to live according to the will of God, or if he desires to do his own thing. The prayer of a vital, growing Christian is, "Make me know Thy ways, oh Lord, teach me Thy paths" (Psalm 25:4). Jesus taught us to pray, "Thy kingdom come, Thy will be done, on earth as it is in heaven," so we should be seeking to establish God's kingdom, not ours.

Beyond Being Willing

Once our will is bent in the right direction, Jesus raises the additional question of motive: "He who speaks from himself, seeks his own glory, but he who is seeking the Glory of the one Who sent him, he is true and there is no unrighteousness in him" (John 7:18). The person who is true glorifies the one who sent him.

This is perfectly modeled in the Godhead. Notice first the example of Jesus: "For I proceeded forth and have come from God, for I have not even come on My own initiative, but He sent Me" (John 8:42). In talking with His Father, Jesus said:

> I glorified Thee on the earth, having accomplished the work which Thou hast given Me to do.... Now they have come to know that everything Thou hast given Me is from Thee; for the words which Thou gavest Me I have given to them; and they received them, and truly understood that I came forth from Thee, and they believed that Thou didst send Me (John 17:4,7,8).

The Holy Spirit acts in the same way. In John 14:16 Jesus said, "I will ask the Father and He will give you another Helper that He may be with you forever, that is the Spirit of Truth." When the Holy Spirit came, this is what He would do:

> When He, the Spirit of Truth comes, He will guide you into all truth, for He will not speak on His own initiative; whatever He will speak, He will speak and disclose to you what is to come. And He shall glorify Me, for He shall take of Mine and shall disclose it to you (John 16:13,14).

I can take this one step further. Are you ready for this? Jesus said in John 20:21, "As the Father has sent Me, I also send you." Granted, that was said to the apostles, but we are all under the Great Commission. Do you want to be true? Then glorify the one who sent you! Paul asked:

> Do you not know your body is a temple of the Holy Spirit Who is in you, Whom you have from God, and that you are not your own? For you have been bought with a price, therefore glorify God in your body (1 Corinthians 6:19,20).

People who know they are God-sent and are committed to live like that, glorify God. Self-sent people seek their own glory.

I know this is a tremendous struggle for those of you who are hurting. You are saying to me, "God gave me lousy parents. I have no money for a decent education. I've been mistreated by others my whole life. And God wants me to sit around and stroke His ego!"

How do we give glory to another when we are desperately looking for affirmation ourselves? Why should we be excited about glorifying God if we believe that it is God who dealt us a bad hand? Does the Bible teach a worm theology, where God is everything and we are nothing? How is God glorified if His children are required to grovel in some pitiful existence? No wonder the New Age teaching that "You are God and all you have to do is realize it" is very attractive to those who have been beaten down by life.

The Cry of the Hurting

I have spent thousands of hours with hurting people who were longing to hear from God. To many of them, the thought of doing the will of God is a tiresome duty with no immediate results. Giving glory to God seems like bowing to a king who demands homage from the poor peasants forced to scramble for the crumbs that fall from his table. Give glory to God! For what?

Let me tell you about someone. If I were to pick the top ten prospects who graduated from our seminary in the last decade, this man would be one of them. He was an excellent student and an outstanding communicator with a winsome personality. Upon graduation he accepted the challenge of a small pastorate, but within two years he was out of the ministry. Two more years passed and God called him back into a pastorate, at which time he attended one of my conferences. Several months after the conference, he wrote me this letter:

> I've always figured I was just a no-good, rotten, dirty, stinking sinner, saved by grace yet failing God miserably every day. And all I could look forward to was a lifetime of apologizing every night for not being the man I know He wants me to be. "I'll try harder tomorrow, Lord."
>
> As a firstborn son, I spent my life trying to earn the approval of highly expectant parents. I've related to God the same way. I felt He just couldn't love me as much as other, "better" believers. Oh sure, I'm saved by grace through faith, but I'm just hanging on until He gets tired of putting up with me here and takes me home to finally stop the failure in progress. Whew, what a treadmill!
>
> Neil, when you said that in our new identification in Christ we're not sinners but saints, you totally blew me away. Isn't that strange, that a guy could go through a good seminary and never latch on to the truth that he is a new creation in Christ?
>
> This has been so helpful and liberating to me. I'm beginning to grow out of my old ways of thinking about myself and about God. I don't constantly picture Him as disappointed in me anymore. If He can still love me, be active in me and find use for even me, after I've failed Him as badly as I have, then surely my worth to Him can't be based on my performance. He just plain loves me. Period.
>
> What a new joyful walk I'm experiencing with Him. Praise God. I have been so deeply touched by the realization of who I am in Christ that I am taking our people through a study in Ephesians to learn who we are in Christ and what we have as believers in Christ. My preaching is different, and our people are profiting greatly by being built up in strength and confidence. I can't tell you how gracious the Lord has been to me, allowing me to try again. Each day of service is a direct gift from God, and I bank each one carefully in heaven's vault for all eternity to the honor and glory of my Savior.

Give glory to God because He can restore and renew the life of a hurting person.

It was my privilege to spend a Saturday morning with a

sharp couple who had driven several hundred miles in the hopes that I could resolve a conflict going on in their home. He was a successful man—a superintendent in a public school district. He attended church regularly and, by all external evidence, appeared to be normal. But he was struggling with compulsive thoughts, explosive anger and incredible nightmares that left him depleted every morning. Within hours we were able to resolve his spiritual conflicts and he found freedom in Christ.

Several months later, being assured that what had happened was lasting, he wrote me a letter. I'd like to share part of it with you:

> I never really understood the relationship God wanted to have with me. I saw God as an omnipotent but distant and stern father. You helped me to realize that God is like a real father in how He loves me, meaning that He wants me to enjoy His presence and live a fulfilling life on this earth. I used to see Him as an aloof disciplinarian, a benevolent disciplinarian, but nevertheless a disciplinarian. I knew that I was to have a personal relationship with Him, but I had no way of knowing what that meant.

> I equated my own earthly father's attitude toward a father/son relationship to the kind of kinship that would be appropriate between God and myself. I was dead wrong. God not only wants to see me obediently happy, but He also takes joy in my accomplishments. I have struggled with my purpose in life. What did it matter whether I achieved anything? If all my achievements were the result of God's will, and all the credit belonged to Him, it followed in my small mind that I was nothing but a non-efficacious vessel of the Almighty.

> Of course I was willing to accept that concept, as I believed it to be biblical. But I was wrong, and I was basing my belief system on a non-scriptural foundation. My downfall was inevitable. There was no way I could experience happiness with this belief. Humility was very important to me. It meant taking no personal satisfaction for a job well done. Without some sort of personal satisfaction for one's endeavors, much of life is missed, and God does not want this. He wants me to do good things and take pleasure in doing them well. Just as an earthly father is pleased when his son does well, so too is God pleased when His children do His will.

> This revelation instilled a great deal of meaning in my

life. I now have a new concept of God's love and my place in His divine plan. I have meaning, and what I do has meaning. I can take pleasure in doing good without risking the sin of pride. Now I see the truth—that God is a loving and caring Father. He gave me a will that I am supposed to use to please Him, and that is exactly what I intend to do.

If God is a consuming fire, you're going to stay away. But if He's a loving Father, you're going to draw near. Your motive for serving Him is not to gain His approval; you're already approved. We don't perform for Him in order to be accepted; we are already accepted. Therefore, we joyfully serve Him. We don't labor in the vineyard so that someday He may notice us and hopefully love us. God has known us from the foundation of the world, and He already loves us. Christians will instinctively give glory to God when they know what God has freely bestowed upon them.

God's Glory Revealed

So what is the glory of God? And how do we glorify God in our body? To begin with, the answer is not joining a health club with the hope that we will acquire the affirmation of others. It's not running endless miles every day, or eating the perfect foods or dieting to the point where we look like an emaciated model. If we do that, who gets the glory?

Don't get me wrong. I believe we're to take care of the temple that houses the Holy Spirit, but not for the sake of drawing attention to ourselves. According to 1 Corinthians 9:27, we are to buffet our body and make it our slave so as not to be disqualified from preaching. In other words, don't lose your witness and ability to serve because you don't take care of yourself. Your body is to serve you, not the other way around.

The glory of God is the manifestation of His presence. In the Old Testament, Moses said, "I pray Thee, show me Thy glory" (Exodus 33:18). God did give Moses a sense of His glory. He said:

> You cannot see My face, for no man can see Me and live.
> . . . Behold there is a place by Me and you shall stand there on
> the rock. And it will come about that when My glory is passing
> by, that I will put you in the cleft of the rock and cover you with

My hand, until I have passed by. Then I will take My hand away and you shall see My back, but My face will not be seen (Exodus 33:20-23).

God also manifested His presence over the Ark of the Covenant in the Holy of Holies:

And the Lord said to Moses, "Tell your brother Aaron that he shall not enter at any time the holy place inside the veil, before the mercy seat which is on the Ark lest he die, for I will appear in the cloud over the mercy seat" (Leviticus 16:2).

The progressive departure of the glory of God is revealed in the book of Ezekiel. In Ezekiel 8:4-6, the glory is present in Jerusalem. In Ezekiel 9:3, the glory of God moves to the threshold of the temple, then returns to the sanctuary. In Ezekiel 10:4, the glory moves back to the threshold. In 10:18,19, the glory moves to the east gate. Then in Ezekiel 11:23 the glory of the Lord goes up from the midst of the city and stands over the mountain which is east of the city. Then, "Ichabod"—the glory departs. Four hundred silent years for Israel begin.

The glory of God doesn't appear again until we read in John 1:14: "And the Word became flesh and dwelt among us, and we beheld His glory, glory as of the only begotten from the Father, full of grace and truth." Jesus was a manifestation of the presence of God. That's why He could say, "He who has seen Me, has seen the Father" (John 14:9). Now we glorify God by manifesting His presence: "By this is my Father glorified, that you bear much fruit, and so prove to be my disciples" (John 15:8).

Right Behavior for People of God

The world system in which we were raised says that we are nothing, so compete, scheme, achieve and get ahead. The biblical system teaches that we are something, so be submissive. Here's how Peter said it:

And coming to Him as to a living stone, rejected by men but choice and precious in the sight of God. . . . But you are a chosen race, a royal priesthood, a holy nation, a people for God's own possession that you may proclaim the excellencies of Him Who has called you out of darkness into His marvelous light. For you once were not a people, but now you are the

people of God. You had not received mercy, but now you have
received mercy (1 Peter 2:4,9,10).

Only after that affirmation of us being the people of God
does Peter say, "Submit yourselves, for the Lord's sake, to every
human institution" (verse 13), and "Servants be submissive to
your masters" (verse 18). He even relates it to the home: "In the
same way you wives be submissive to your own husbands" (1
Peter 3:1).

Do I believe in the depravity of man? I certainly do. I believe
I was utterly dead in my trespasses and sins, separated from God,
and there was nothing I could do about it. I had nothing to look
forward to but a godless eternity. God took the initiative and,
praise Him, I'm not depraved anymore! I'm a child of God, and
so are all born-again believers.

One of my students wrote me this note:

> What really struck me was the concept that we are saints
> and not sinners. I remember how surprised I was when I took
> Greek and saw that a Christian is often called *hagios* ("holy
> one"). I was so steeped in the idea that I was a totally depraved
> sinner. The concept of who we are in Christ didn't break
> through until I read your book *Victory Over the Darkness*.
>
> I'm still adjusting to the lofty concept that my real self is
> holy instead of wretched. I have been saved more than twelve
> years, and I have never really appreciated what happened to
> me at my conversion. I always knew that my future destiny
> was secure, but I didn't understand that I was truly a brand
> new creation in Christ Jesus.

Why Live Below Your Privilege?

I love the illustration Bob George gives in his book *Classic
Christianity*. Suppose you are a prostitute. One day you hear that
the king has decreed that all prostitutes are forgiven. Since you're
a prostitute, that's great news! But would it necessarily change
your behavior or your self-perception? Probably not. You may
dance in the streets for awhile, but chances are you would
continue in your same vocation. You would see yourself as
nothing more than a forgiven prostitute.

Now suppose the king not only forgave you, but he made

you his bride as well. You're a queen. Would that change your behavior? Of course. Why would you want to live as a prostitute if you were the queen?

The church is the bride of Christ! You are far more likely to promote the kingdom if you are the queen rather than a forgiven prostitute. We are not redeemed caterpillars; we are butterflies. Why would you want to crawl in some false humility when you are called to mount up with wings as eagles?

"I would be filled with pride if I believed that," says the skeptic. You are defeated if you don't believe it! Humility is not putting yourself down when God is trying to build you up. Self-abasement has the appearance of wisdom, but it has no value against fleshly indulgence according to Colossians 2:23. Humility is confidence properly placed. We need to be like Paul and "put no confidence in the flesh" (Philippians 3:3). Let's put our confidence in God: "For it is God working in you both to will and to work for His good pleasure" (Philippians 2:13).

A sharp student at Talbot shared that he struggled with a poor sense of self-worth. Finding out who he was in Christ became the primary motivation to seek God and to do His will. He took a couple of lists of Scriptures that I use and rearranged them so he could clearly understand that he was significant, accepted and secure in Christ. Whenever he felt low or questioned his worth, he would read through the list. Let me share his list with you:

IN CHRIST

I AM SIGNIFICANT:

Matthew 5:13	I am the salt of the earth.
Matthew 5:14	I am the light of the earth.
John 1:12	I am God's child (Romans 8:14-16; 1 John 3:1-3).
John 15:1,5	I am a branch of the true vine, a channel of His life.
John 15:16	I have been chosen and appointed to bear fruit.
Acts 1:8	I am a personal witness of Christ's.
1 Corinthians 3:16	I am God's temple.

1 Corinthians 12:27	I am a member of Christ's body.
2 Corinthians 5:17,18	I am a minister of reconciliation for God.
2 Corinthians 6:1	I am God's co-worker (1 Corinthians 3:9).
Ephesians 1:1	I am a saint.
Ephesians 2:6	I have been raised up and I am seated with Christ.
Ephesians 2:10	I am God's workmanship.
Philippians 3:20	I am a citizen of heaven (Ephesians 2:6).

I AM ACCEPTED:

John 15:15	I am Christ's friend.
Romans 5:1	I have been justified.
1 Corinthians 6:17	I am joined to the Lord and I am one spirit with Him.
1 Corinthians 6:20	I have been bought with a price. I belong to God.
1 Corinthians 12:27	I am a member of Christ's body.
2 Corinthians 5:21	I have been made righteous.
Ephesians 1:5	I have been adopted as God's child.
Ephesians 2:18	I have direct access to God through the Holy Spirit.
Ephesians 2:19	I am of God's household.
Ephesians 2:19	I am a fellow citizen with the rest of the saints.
Ephesians 3:12	I may approach God with boldness and confidence.
Colossians 1:14	I have been redeemed and forgiven of all my sins.
Colossians 2:10	I am complete in Christ.

I AM SECURE:

John 1:12	I am a child of God (Galatians 3:26-28).
Romans 8:28	I am assured that all things work together for good.
Romans 8:35	I cannot be separated from the love of God.
Romans 8:1	I am free forever from condemnation.
Romans 8:33	I am free from any condemning charges against me.
2 Corinthians 1:21	I have been established, anointed and sealed by God.

Ephesians 1:13,14	I have been given the Holy Spirit as a pledge, guaranteeing my inheritance to come.
Colossians 1:13	I have been delivered from the domain of darkness and transferred to the kingdom of Christ.
Colossians 3:3	I am hidden with Christ in God.
Philippians 1:6	I am confident that the good work that God has begun in me will be perfected.
Philippians 4:13	I can do all things through Him who strengthens me.
2 Timothy 1:7	I have not been given a spirit of fear, but of power, love and a sound mind.
Hebrews 4:16	I can find grace and mercy in time of need.
1 John 5:1	I am born of God and the evil one cannot touch me.

Those verses aren't true because of what you and I have done. They are true because of what Christ has done. Knowing who we are becomes a primary motivation of wanting to serve God. Listen to Paul's testimony in 1 Corinthians 15:10:

> But by the grace of God I am what I am, and His grace toward me did not prove vain, but I labored even more than all of them, yet not I but the grace of God in me.

I'm convinced that we will "labor even more" when we understand the tremendous position we have in Christ.

A pastor's wife attended my conference on "Resolving Personal and Spiritual Conflicts." She discovered who she was as a child of God and found her freedom in Christ. She wrote, "I crave to share Jesus with people out of my own love for Him, whereas before it was largely an 'I should' activity."

A seminary student stopped by my office and told me he was changing his major from missions to practical theology. He said, "My motivation to go into missions was to gain God's approval. I suppose it was a carry-over from my childhood days because I'd never been able to live up to my father's expectations." The following summer he participated in a short-term missions program. When he got back he made another appointment to see me. He said, "I'm changing my major back to missions. But now I'm going not because I have to, but because I want to." Only a liberated child of God whose identity is firmly established in Christ joyfully gives glory to God and seeks to establish His kingdom.

Let's stop trying to become something we already are. That can only lead to futility. If we refuse to accept who we are, then no amount of self-effort or works on our part can possibly result in freedom from our hurt. We labor for an unattainable goal and God truly becomes a stern taskmaster to us.

But once we see ourselves from God's perspective, and know who we are in Christ, we are then freed to serve our loving heavenly Father. We experience the guiding hand of Him who has sent us and are able to freely live to the glory of God.

Hurting people . . . the world is filled with hurting people. People who suffer injustices as well as the consequences of their own bad choices. People who, in their struggle for freedom from their hurt, focus on causes outside of themselves and others to blame, including God. But to those who hurt, God offers a total release. As we seek to glorify Him, He will manifest His glory in us. Would you pray with me for this reality in your life?

Loving Father, I would ask like Moses, "Show me Your glory." I desire for Your presence to be manifested in this world. I ask You to fill me with Your Spirit that I may glorify You in my body. Forgive me for the times that I have sought my own glory and acted independently from You.

Thank You for giving me life and calling me Your child. I declare my dependency upon You. I want nothing more than to reflect Your image as I grow in Christ-likeness.

I commit myself to seek no other glory but Yours. You are the only One deserving all honor, glory and praise. I lift up the name of Jesus and pray that You will draw all men to Him. I will work from this day forward by Your grace to establish Your Kingdom. You are the king of my life. Amen.

A LIGHT TO MY PATH

I have fond childhood memories of playing the board game Monopoly with my younger sister—probably because I always won!

I'm sure we initially read the directions and attempted to play by the rules. However, every time we played, the rules changed according to our personal desires. Not only that, but I must confess my deviousness in persuading my sister to make trades of property. I would make her feel like she was getting a terrific deal when, in fact, I was the one who came out ahead. Sibling rivalry and family tradition gradually set aside the rules of the game while the motive of the players grew increasingly suspect.

Such was the case of the Jewish community at the time of Christ. But the game they were playing had eternal significance. Their traditions had set aside the commandments of God and gone beyond being devious by imposing legalistic behavior on their followers to keep them in bondage. Jesus not only revealed their sick motives, but He also established the Word of God as the only authoritative rule that can guide us through the game of life.

Today we need to understand how we have distorted the truth of God's Word and/or set it aside for the sake of church or family traditions or personal comfort. Jesus confronted the issue when He was attacked by the Jews for healing on the Sabbath and accused of having a demon:

> "Did not Moses give you the law, and yet none of you carries out the law? Why do you seek to kill Me?" The multitude answered, "You have a demon. Who seeks to kill You?" Jesus answered and said to them, "I did one deed, and you all marvel. On this account Moses has given you circumcision (not because it is from Moses, but from the fathers), and on the Sabbath you circumcise a man. If a man receives circumcision on the Sabbath that the Law of Moses may not be broken, are you angry with Me because I made an entire man well on the Sabbath?" (John 7:19-23)

Regarding the Sabbath issue, Jesus argued that the Mosaic law required circumcision on the eighth day. If a child was born eight days before the Sabbath, then the law required that he be circumcised on the Sabbath. If it is lawful to circumcise a child on the Sabbath, why not bring healing to the whole person on that day? If Scripture is interpreted wrongly, it will be applied wrongly.

Jesus said, "You nicely set aside the commandment of God in order to keep your tradition" (Mark 7:9). Jesus was never one to beat around the bush. In essence He was saying, "Moses gave you the rule book, and none of you are following it! Not only that, but some of you are seeking to kill Me." The last charge was a fact recorded earlier in John 5:18: "For this cause, therefore, the Jews were seeking all the more to kill Him, because He not only was breaking the Sabbath, but also was calling God His own Father, making Himself equal with God."

The accusation that Jesus had a demon resulted from the Israelites' bewilderment that Jesus could discern the nature of their hearts. Blinded to the truth, they concluded that Jesus received His information from a demonic source. I think it is interesting to note that the early church also believed Satan was capable of putting thoughts into our minds. Let the modern church not be ignorant of the warning in 1 Timothy 4:1: "But the Spirit explicitly says that in the latter times some will fall away from the faith, paying attention to deceitful spirits and doctrines [teachings] of demons."

God's View of False Guidance

Let me illustrate from the Bible God's attitude toward those who would turn to the occult for guidance instead of the living God and His Word.

When King Ahaziah of Israel fell through the lattice in his upper chamber, he sent messengers to inquire of Baal-zebub, the god of Ekron, whether he was going to recover from his sickness. But the angel of the Lord said to Elijah, "Arise, go up to meet the messengers of the king of Samaria and say to them, 'Is it because there is no god in Israel that you are going to inquire of Baal-zebub the god of Ekron?' " (2 Kings 1:3) The message he did receive from God was that he would surely die, and die he did.

Isaiah 8:19,20 records:

> And when they say to you, "Consult the mediums and the spiritists who whisper and mutter," should not a people consult their God? Should they consult the dead on behalf of the living? To the law and to the testimony! If they do not speak according to this word, it is because they have no dawn.

Even though the Hebrew nation had the law and the prophets, their history abounds with leaders seeking false gods, turning away from the commandments of Moses, not heeding the warnings of the prophets and severely distorting the true intent of the Word of God.

In the New Testament, Jesus affirmed the validity of the law and the prophets and warned against distorting that truth. He said in Matthew 5:17-19:

> Do not think that I came to abolish the law or the prophets; I did not come to abolish, but to fulfill. For truly I say to you, until heaven and earth pass away, not the smallest letter or stroke shall pass away from the law, until all is accomplished. Whoever then annuls one of the least of these commandments, and so teaches others, shall be called least in the kingdom of heaven; but whoever keeps and teaches them, he shall be called great in the kingdom of heaven.

We are warned in James 3:1, "Let not many of you become teachers, my brethren, knowing that as such we shall incur a stricter judgment." The Bible warns of severe penalties for those who would distort its meaning since it is the only infallible source for understanding the will of God.

Matthew 23 reveals that Jesus considered the religious establishment of His day as the least in the kingdom of God, calling its leaders (among many other things) "blind guides" (verse 24). The Pharisees sat themselves in the seat of Moses (verse 2) and thus shut off the kingdom of heaven from men (verse 13).

Rightly Using God's Word

It goes beyond the scope of this book to tackle the problem of hermeneutics (principles of biblical interpretation). I do want to identify several issues, however, that affect the way we understand and apply the Bible to life. From that we'll see how we stray into error—and fall prey to Satan's half-truths and lies.

First, if our interpretation of Scripture is going to be right, it must be *systematic*. Individual parts need to be seen in the context of the whole. There are two potential hindrances which keep our theology from being systematic.

1. *Many Christians don't see the whole picture.* They come to church weekly and receive a piece of the puzzle. Occasionally they miss a week, so most don't even have all the pieces. Imagine how difficult it would be to put a puzzle together without the picture on the box. Individual pieces remain disassociated from the whole.

2. *We view the picture through the grid of our own limited perspective.* In conferences, I'll have a volunteer come forward to illustrate this point. Holding up my hand with the palm facing me, I'll ask the volunteer to describe what he sees. Eventually, he'll get to the fingernails, and I'll protest, "Wait a minute. There are no fingernails on this hand. How can you say there are fingernails when I don't see any? Are we looking at the same hand?" We are looking at the same hand, but from different perspectives.

Truth has many dimensions. In order to perceive the whole truth we need to accept the other person's perspective. That's why there are four Gospels. All four wrote about the life, death, burial and resurrection of Christ. All four are different. Which one is the correct perspective? All four! If you want a complete picture, you have to read all four.

When I first got married, I thought it was important (being the head of the home) that the right perspective would bear light on all issues. Of course that perspective was mine. Then I matured a little and tolerated my wife's perspective. Then I matured a little more and appreciated my wife's perspective. Then I matured a little more and began to seek it out.

Let me illustrate. If my son Karl fell down and scratched his knee when he was a baby, my wife's first response was, "Oh, poor baby!" My response was, "Get up. Be a man!" Twenty years later when Karl scratches his knee my wife says, "Oh, poor baby, get up." And I respond, "Get up, poor baby." We've been influenced by each other's perspective, and it has affected how we respond to life.

The tragedy of our time is that few intellectuals admit to their bias. Dispensationalists remain dispensational. Covenant theologians remain covenant in their understanding of Scripture. And Catholics remain Catholic. There's nothing wrong with having distinctives, if we are open to hearing other perspectives. One of my privileges is to teach at an interdenominational school in Southern California where cultural pluralism abounds. While this setting helps purge out traditions that no longer serve a purpose, there is a limit to what we can tolerate. It's one thing to disagree with another's interpretation; it's another to question whether the Bible is the only authoritative source for faith and practice.

Second, to have a biblical hermeneutic, we must adhere to a *grammatical, historical method of biblical interpretation.* How does this apply as we study the Bible? We must understand how the Bible was put together.

1. *God has revealed Himself in time and space.* I have traveled twice to Israel. There is a Jerusalem, a temple, a Jordan River and a Sea of Galilee. The basis for the Christian faith is rooted in geography and history. History is His story fleshed out in our three-dimensional world. This is not the case with many cults which base their faith in mystical time and space.

2. *The self-disclosure of God was an unfolding process.* It oc-

curred over a time span of 1400 years. It wasn't complete until John received his vision on the island of Patmos, resulting in the book of Revelation. Historical Christianity has accepted the fact that the canon (the number of books that belong in the Bible) is closed. There is no new revelation of scriptural quality. Although God is certainly guiding His church through the presence of the indwelling Holy Spirit, no present guidance from God will be contrary to His will already revealed in Scripture.

The Holy Spirit is first and foremost the Spirit of truth (John 14:17). Jesus said, "When He, the Spirit of Truth, comes, He will guide you into all truth" (John 16:13). When Jesus prayed, He said, "I do not ask Thee to take them out of the world, but to keep them from the evil one" (John 17:15). Then He says, "Sanctify them in the truth, Thy Word is truth" (verse 17). The primary function of the Holy Spirit is to establish God's presence in our lives and enable us to understand the Word of God.

Most conservative biblical scholars do not believe the Bible was dictated by God in the sense that God told human sources what to write by some audible means. That would be like the occultic practice of automatic writing which requires the writer to function as a medium. An occultic medium or a New Age channeler functions by assuming a passive state of the mind. Instead, God worked through the minds of the prophets and apostles and superintended the choice of words. We have a reliable text inspired by God with the personalities of the writers coming through.

In a similar fashion, the guidance of God does not bypass our responsibility to think or to search the Scriptures. We need to be like the Bereans who were considered "noble-minded" because they examined the Scriptures daily to see if these things were so (Acts 17:11).

3. *The grammatical, historical method of interpretation requires that we understand what it meant to the hearers at that time,* in their language and their culture. A similar need exists today when missionaries struggle with the problem of contextualization (translating the Bible and biblical truth in the context of the culture). Missionaries need to isolate the truth of God's Word from their own cultural bias and rightly apply it to the culture in

which they are ministering. Truth is transcultural and, if understood correctly, is true for all people at all times.

4. *The fourth requirement of an historical, grammatical method of interpretation is to understand the literary context.* Nothing has meaning without context. Who was the book written to, and why was it written? What is the major point of the passage under consideration? Never isolate a passage, text, sentence or word from its literary context. There is only one true interpretation. However, there may be many applications.

Why We Misunderstand the Bible

While God has given us an infallible guide to life—His Word—the truth He wants us to follow for our freedom can be obscured by our bias and selfish indulgence. In the twentieth-century Western church, I see at least five major hindrances which affect our understanding and application of the Word of God.

First, *there is a tendency to make doctrine an end in itself.* A major problem in Christian education is having the wrong goal. Christian maturity is not understanding principles of the Bible; Christian maturity is character. According to 1 Timothy 1:5, "The goal of our instruction is love from a pure heart, a good conscience, and a sincere faith." If our doctrine is right, it will govern our relationship with God and man. If what we come to accept as truth doesn't affect our love for God and man, something is radically wrong. Knowledge "makes arrogant, but love edifies" (1 Corinthians 8:1).

Second, *we can learn a lot about God from Scripture and not know Him at all.* Before his conversion, Paul knew the law, but he didn't recognize God in Christ when he saw Him. After Paul was struck down by the Lord on the Damascus Road, his life pursuit was, "I count all things to be loss in view of the surpassing value of knowing Christ Jesus my Lord" (Philippians 3:8). We're not asked to fall in love with doctrine. We're to fall in love with the Lord Jesus Christ.

Third, *we often encourage memorizing Scripture instead of thinking scripturally.* Rote memory without integration is a Western world concept of learning. Our model should be, "The Word became flesh and dwelt amongst us." We are to incarnate the Word of God. We are to have our lives transformed by it, and our minds renewed by it. We need to integrate truth into the very fabric of our lives, not simply memorize it.

Fourth, *we often hear the Word and then don't do it.* The Western world concept of education is characterized by acquiring data. The Hebrew concept was determined by obedience. For instance, the Great Commission requires us to go into the world, making disciples and teaching them to observe all that Christ commanded. It's in the observation (obedience) that we learn and not in the hearing. The will of God is thwarted by educating people beyond their obedience. Jesus taught, "If you know these things, blessed are you if you do them" (John 13:17). James expanded on the idea:

> But the one who looks intently at the perfect law, the law of liberty, and abides by it, not having become a forgetful hearer, but an effectual doer, this man shall be blessed in what he does (James 1:25).

Fifth, like the Pharisees, *we tend to "neglect the commandment of God, and hold to the tradition of man"* (Mark 7:8). I believe this is one of the most serious problems affecting our churches today. Many of our graduates leave seminary with a desire to serve God and bear fruit for His glory. They labor in their last year to discern God's guidance. Many fear that there will be no "call." Most are young and filled with idealism. I fear the possibility that their first "call" may come from an old wineskin (a church rooted in the traditions of men), and we send them out as new wine (zealous to serve God according to the truth of His Word).

A Timeless Message for a Changing Culture

The world at the end of the twentieth century is changing at an alarming rate. People are under tremendous stress to keep up with the rapid rate of change. The ecclesiastical challenge is to give anxious people the timeless message of Christ and present it in a contemporary way that relates to a changing culture.

Many of the older and mature saints who rightfully constitute the boards and committees in our traditional evangelical churches resist change. They are comfortable with the form of worship, style of music and methods of teaching that brought them to Christ and helped them mature. They get uncomfortable when a young pastor comes in with new ideas and a desire to change their Christian practices. I, myself, am deeply committed to the authority of Scripture and desire to see both the old and the new wine preserved, so I offer these comments as God seeks to guide us into the twenty-first century.

Jesus not only came to fulfill the law, but He also came to usher in a new age. The Jewish community was locked into tradition. Most of the opposition to Jesus didn't come when He presented the truth, but when He confronted their traditions. When one doesn't conform to the customs and practices of the status quo, the establishment will be offended. The new wine often comes under the scrutiny, and sometimes the wrath, of the old wineskins.

Jesus was taking bold steps in the process of change and such steps are by far the most perilous. Machiavelli wrote in *The Prince*, "There is nothing more difficult to take in hand, more perilous to conduct, or more uncertain in its success, than to take the lead in the introduction of a new order of things."

In my first pastorate, I had the privilege of leading our church from rented facilities to the acquisition of new property and buildings. That was only one of many changes that as a young pastor I attempted to bring about. Others included a revision in the constitution that changed the form of our church government. And while the preceding pastor was formal and conservative in style, I advocated more freedom of expression and contemporary worship.

The board members I worked with were at least twenty years my senior, and most were charter members. Many of them would agree that the new property and government were better than what we had before, but when I left the church I had "bullet holes" all over my body!

I can give you a different, more refreshing experience. More recently I had the privilege of helping an established church through an organizational change. The pastor had been there for thirty years and had led the church from its beginning to more than 1000 attenders. The organization had evolved with little planning or purpose, so we reorganized twenty-six committees into seven. Although the organizational change was significant, it took place without any dissension. The major key in this case was the cooperation and credibility of the pastor.

If God is leading us into the twenty-first century, we must learn how to adapt our ministry to a changing culture. But while we do, there are some biblical criteria that Jesus taught and modeled that must shape our thinking as we consider revising established practices. Let's look at the example of Christ and see how He responded to Pharisaic traditions that conflicted with the Scriptures.

When Not to Conform to Pharisaic Practices

One of the beautiful things about Jesus is His universal appeal. If you are an ultraconservative, it will thrill your heart to know that He changes not: "Jesus Christ is the same yesterday and today, yes and forever" (Hebrews 13:8). If you are a flaming liberal, you will love the way He refused to participate in Pharisaic practices, particularly the customary traditions of fasting, ritual washings and observing the Sabbath.

The Gospels reveal the conflict that arises when truth, purpose and meaning are at odds with tradition. The fact that Jesus was willing to suffer the rejection of the establishment clearly shows that there is something greater at stake than simply getting one's own way. There are three criteria by which we should determine when a stand for truth should be made against church traditions:

1. Don't conform if the traditions place people under an unnecessary burden (Luke 11:37-41).

The law of Moses called for cleansing after touching an unclean animal or contact with a corpse and ceremonial cleansings for religious practices. To those laws the Rabbis added many petty little rules to guard against every possible defilement. Hygiene was no longer the issue—purification was. They reasoned, "If we have contact with anything impure, we are impure, and therefore we must be cleansed by washing." The water must also be pure and if the water must be pure then the vessel carrying the water must be pure, and so forth.

The *Talmud*, a collection of ancient Rabbinic writings, relates the story of Rabbi Akiba who was imprisoned. Rabbi Joshua brought him some water but the guard spilled half of the container. There was too little water to both wash and drink and Rabbi Akiba faced the possibility of death for lack of water if he chose to wash. He reasoned, "He who eats with unwashed hands perpetuates a crime that ought to be punished by death. Better for me to die of thirst than to transgress the traditions of my ancestors!"

Any preoccupation with trifles as matters of conscience will make one either a moral imbecile or an intolerable hypocrite. Jesus responded harshly to such reasoning: "You blind guides who strain out a gnat and swallow a camel!" (Matthew 23:24) The Lord cautions that the weightier matters of the law (such as justice and mercy) are overlooked when attention focuses on strict observance of religious practices. This leads to a corresponding negligence of the eternal laws of God. Jesus told the people to pay more attention to cleansing their hearts and not be like their leaders who cleanse only their hands.

The laws of God are liberating and protective. They are restrictive only when they protect us from the evil one. The rules of any institution should ensure the freedom of each individual to reach their God-given potential. They should serve as a guide so we don't stray from our purpose, and they should protect us from those who abuse the system.

The principle that Jesus modeled could be stated as follows: If people are commanded to follow a traditional practice that makes life more difficult and no longer contributes to the purpose of the organization, then we must not participate as a matter of religious conscience. Jesus simply didn't observe such traditions, and He defended His disciples for not observing them as well.

2. Don't conform if the traditions distort the law they are intended to serve (Luke 6:1-11).

In His ministry, Jesus often violated the traditional instructions surrounding the observance of the Sabbath because they were a clear distortion of God's commandment. A common practice, born out of a desire to protect a known law or principle, is to establish additional rules to keep us from breaking the laws or violating the principles. We establish fences around the laws, but within a short time the fences become laws.

For instance, we are not to be unequally yoked (2 Corinthians 6:14,15). To ensure that this doesn't happen, we sometimes build a fence around the law by establishing additional rules such as, "You can't associate with or date a non-Christian." That may be advisable in some cases, but don't make it a law. Some have gone to the extreme by requiring that their children never associate with non-Christians. This makes the Great Commission a formidable task!

Here's another example. A common practice in many churches, left over from the Prohibition era, is to require total abstinence from alcohol. Again, that may be wise in many cases, but the Bible instructs against strong drink and drunkenness and teaches us to do all things in moderation. The major biblical concern is not the alcohol, but whether we're being a stumbling block to a weaker brother. Total abstinence may actually keep some from the medicine they need or it may be detrimental when relating to a weaker brother.

I was confronted by this last point when a neighbor whom I had led to Christ found out I was home with a terrible cold. She came by that evening with a "hot toddy" to cure me. Being a Baptist pastor, did I accept this act of love? I'll leave you with the tension of not knowing what I did, but I will admit to this—I slept like a baby that night!

The point is, we can easily distort the true Word of God by adding our own traditional practices and making them equal with the original intent of God. We may need to stand against Pharisaic practices as the Lord did—before we find ourselves in bondage to man-made traditions.

3. Don't conform if the traditions are contrary to the will of God (Mark 7:6-9).

Time devoted solely to the traditions of man is often morally corrupt time. Out of necessity there is a corresponding decrease in the commitment to the commandments of God for every commitment to the traditions of man. Remember, "You nicely set aside the commandment of God in order to keep your tradition" (Mark 7:9). It is easy to see this in others, yet very difficult to see it in ourselves. Santa Claus at Christmas and the Easter Bunny at Easter are obvious, but what isn't obvious are the little traditions that churches and Christians keep observing year after year, although their purpose is no longer evident.

We cannot ignore the clear example of Jesus. If the Word of God is being abused or distorted in any way, if traditional practices no longer serve their purpose or add to the burdens of people, we must take an active stand.

Changing Christian Practices for Effective Ministry

I really don't mind taking a stand on biblical grounds and living with the conflict that comes from those who oppose the gospel. I think that is part of our calling. What grieves God is when our ministry and work is stopped because well-intentioned people resist the inevitable and needlessly fight change.

I tell my students that the greatest asset they will have in their early years of ministry is older mature saints in the church. The greatest liability they will have is old saints who stopped growing years ago. All these saints want to do is censor. They reflect no more love or kindness now than they did twenty years ago. They don't worship—they critique the worship service. They no longer sit under the judgment of Scripture—they sit in judgment of the pastor. They no longer bear fruit—they actually prevent it. They insist that they are right when what they need to be is holy.

Another problem arises when Christian leaders act impulsively as change agents without giving thought to what the consequences will be to the fellowship. Any movement forward that costs the price of fellowship is too high. We must be diligent to preserve the unity of the Spirit. Such change agents seem to be unaware that patience is a fruit of the Spirit. The modern generation wants it now. They seem to have forgotten the fact that God does everything decently and in order. He is not the author of confusion.

To both groups I offer the following suggestions.

The law had required an annual fast on the Day of Atonement. By the time of Zechariah, there were four days of fasting per year. In Jesus' time, strict Jews were fasting twice a week (Luke 18:12). John's disciples were fasting, but the Lord's disciples weren't. The Pharisees wanted to know why. Jesus used this occasion to share four principles that are timeless and critical for our day. I will be using Luke 5:33-39 to show the process of change:

> And they said to Him, "The disciples of John often fast and offer prayers; the disciples of the Pharisees also do the same; but Yours eat and drink." And Jesus said to them, "You cannot make the attendants of the bridegroom fast while the bridegroom is with them, can you? But the days will come; and when the bridegroom is taken away from them, then they will fast in those days." And He was also telling them a parable: "No one tears a piece from a new garment and puts it on an old garment; otherwise he will both tear the new, and the piece from the new will not match the old. And no one puts new wine into old wineskins; otherwise the new wine will burst the skins, and it will be spilled out, and the skins will be ruined. But new wine must be put into fresh wineskins. And no one, after drinking old wine wishes for new; for he says, 'The old is good enough.' "

1. Jesus taught that Christian practices should be appropriate for the situation.

Jesus doesn't condemn or condone John's disciples. It was all right for John's disciples to fast, and it was all right if Jesus' disciples didn't. The point that Jesus makes is that it isn't necessary for His disciples to fast while He is with them. The day will come when He won't be with them, and then they will fast. It's not a question of ritual, but of purpose.

Determining the purpose, and whether it is appropriate, requires an answer to the question, WHY? "We have always done it this way before" is unacceptable. Christian practices continue for years, often outliving their purpose, until someone asks, "Why do we do that?" Then watch the defenses come up!

For instance, having three church services a week is generally practiced by evangelical Christians, but few know why. Originally, Sunday morning was for instruction and worship. Sunday evening was for evangelism, and the Wednesday service was for prayer. Today few churches have three services for those same purposes. In many churches, evangelism has switched to Sunday morning (if there is an evangelistic service). Sunday evenings range from body life gatherings to an informal repeat of the morning service. (I think the major reason for the decline in Sunday evening attendance is the lack of purpose.) Wednesday stopped being a prayer meeting years ago.

Few people can say why they have an adult fellowship group and, consequently, most never fulfill the greatest purpose for which they exist. Without a clear purpose, planning dribbles down to who is going to be the teacher and what is the next monthly social! The purpose of fellowship groups is to provide a base for incorporating new people into the church, going after those who stray, and meeting the needs of one another. Routine activities that lack purpose produce mindless participation. How is God going to guide such a group?

The greatest avenue for productive change is to clarify the purpose of any existing ministry or group. I sat with the leaders of an adult group and helped them hammer out a purpose statement. Some major changes took place in their class. Within two years they had doubled. Asking "Why?" forced them to evaluate their purpose and ministry, and necessary changes came.

2. Jesus taught that Christian practices should be consistent with the inward condition of the heart.

Holding to external practices which no longer correlate with the heart is repugnant to God. Jesus railed against praying in vain repetitions and putting on a gloomy face while fasting. Consistency cries for an affirmative answer to the question, "Is it real?" The Christian community searches for truth while the world searches for reality. These are large overlapping circles, but I'm convinced that we must be real in order to be right. Change is most needed when Christians sit stoically week after week reciting endless creeds in utter hypocrisy.

Tragically, those who are coming to a church simply to fulfill a religious obligation are the most resistant to change. They have resisted the need to change under the instruction of the Word and are in a state of carnality. They are not coming to the changeless Christ and saying, "Change me so I may be like You."

Paradoxically, the ones who have a real Christian experience are the ones who are free to change their Christian practices. They are committed to the substance of their faith, not the form. Form always follows function, but people have a tendency to fixate on the form. The way to avoid that is to focus on the heart as Jesus did.

Organizational renewal will not bring spiritual renewal. When the spiritual tide is out, every little tadpole wants his own little tide pool to swim in. When the spiritual tide is in, the fish swim in one big ocean where someone is synchronizing every move. When the Holy Spirit is leading, almost any organization will work. But when He isn't, it doesn't matter how good the program and organization is, it won't work.

3. Jesus taught that the forms of our Christian practice must change.

Here the Lord carefully chooses His metaphors. The garment and the wineskins are the external dress and the container, not the substance of our faith. They represent the religious customs, practices and traditions which the substance of our faith is packaged in. Jesus is stating a fact—the garment needs mending and the old wineskin is old! What worked before isn't working anymore. Times change, cultures change and what worked twenty years ago may not work today. But what doesn't change is the object of our faith.

"Time-honored faith" and "long-established practice" blend together and become indistinguishable to the status quo. When someone advocates another form of practice, it becomes painfully apparent that the security of the old wineskins rests in the long-established practice instead of the time-honored faith.

The reasoning behind the resistance is logical: "I came to Christ singing that song," or "It worked for me. I don't see why it won't work for my children." I have sat in worship services all choked up listening to a piece of music or a favorite passage and then noticed that it didn't mean a thing to my children. We have to ask, "Is it relevant? Does it relate?" The older generation is the stable force in our churches. They are faithful and mature, and they represent the financial stability that every church needs. They also make up the boards and committees that determine the style of ministry, and they have a natural tendency to perpetuate the long-established practices because they find them meaningful.

This problem is not spiritual; it's sociological. Why is it that a good Bible-believing church which faithfully carries out its ministry struggles to hold onto its young people, when down the street a contemporary ministry rents a store building and has four times more young people in a matter of months? Because the contemporary ministry relates to the young and their style of music. It caters to their desire for expression and participation. The forty-and-under crowd was raised in a different culture than the forty-and-above. And this brings up the fourth principle.

4. Jesus taught that Christian practices should preserve the old and the new wine.

The old wine is vastly superior to the new. The old wine eulogizes the venerable past and loves to contrast it with the present. Make no mistake: They are wise, gentle, reverent and good. Because of the quality of their vintage, they create a strong prejudice against any proposed change. Even Jesus conceded to loving the old wine of Jewish piety: "And no one, after drinking the old wine wishes for the new; for he says, 'The old wine is good enough.' " But its supply will run out!

New wine can be bitter and harsh in the natural order of things. But can we object to its existence? Can we deny the need for new forms of worship and styles of music, art and even instruction? We may not straightway desire it because it is strange and novel, but wisdom says not to spurn, spill or spoil it.

This last principle asks the question, "Does it unify?" The unity of the Spirit is already present. The task is to instruct believers that it is the responsibility of all to practice unity by tolerating the preferences of others and accepting the diversity of the body as a good thing. The task is difficult, but not impossible.

If we are to accomplish our purpose, we must ask ourselves four questions:

- Why are we doing what we are doing?
- Is it real?
- Does it relate?
- Does it unify?

I believe that God will lead us into the twenty-first century if we are diligent to separate the substance of our faith from its various forms.

If you join me in wanting to be free from personal prejudices and follow the essentials of the faith in a changing world, then would you pray with me?

Dear Heavenly Father, I thank You for Your Word. I ask You to rid me of my biases. I want to know the truth and to see life from Your perspective, not from my limited viewpoint. I want to know You and be conformed to Your image.

Keep me from just being a hearer of the Word and not a doer. I ask You to sort out the Christian practices in my life that are setting aside Your commandments. I don't want to go to church just to go to church. I want to meet together with You and Your children in a real, living fellowship. Show me what I need to do in order for that to happen. I don't want to criticize others and the worship service. I want to love others and to worship You. I don't want to sit in judgment of the message, but let it sit in judgment of me.

Lead me, Lord, through Your Word. Transform my mind so I can prove that Your will is good, acceptable and perfect. Amen.

*What a priceless commodity is the peace
that results from judging rightly the
influences that invade our lives.*

9

A PEACE IN
MY HEART

We live in a world where the flip of a switch instantly lightens or darkens a room. The lamps in biblical times, on the other hand, burned brightly but required proper tending. If not cared for, they would become a dwindling flame. God's Word uses the metaphor of a lamp to teach us about guidance for our lives. And it provides the opportunity for some graphic applications of this teaching.

The psalmist wrote, "Thy word is a lamp to my feet, and a light to my path" (Psalm 119:105). Earnestly seeking the clear teaching of God's Word allows the lamp to burn brightly and us to stay on a straight path. When we fail to acknowledge our theological bias and limited perspective, the light lessens and our path becomes twisted. The lamp flickers when form replaces function and traditions push aside the commandments of God. The light dims when we stay away from God's Word and the fellowship of believers. It goes out when we serve another master.

Sometimes we overlook the obvious: God's will is expressed by His Word. As a child, I didn't struggle with knowing my earthly father's will. He clearly expressed it to me. I learned early on that we lived together peacefully if I was quick to obey. Being a farm boy, it made sense to help my father establish his kingdom (the family farm). Farmers know from nature that we reap what we sow. Not only that, I stood to inherit the family farm along with my brothers and sisters as my father had with his sisters. Yet I wonder how many Christians realize that what they are presently sowing in the kingdom of God is what they will reap for all eternity.

The Need to Know Truth

I have learned from successes and failures that I live peacefully with my heavenly Father when I am quick to obey Him. Jesus said, "If anyone loves Me, he will keep My Word; and My Father will love him, and We will come to him, and make Our abode with Him" (John 14:23). It only makes sense to pray, "Thy kingdom come," because as children of God we are destined to inherit it: "Come, you who are blessed of My Father, inherit the kingdom prepared for you from the foundation of the world" (Matthew 25:34).

But "do you not know that the unrighteous shall not inherit the kingdom of God?" (1 Corinthians 6:9) If righteousness determines our destiny, it is little wonder that Jesus made this further point: "Do not judge according to appearance, but judge with righteous judgment" (John 7:24).

Using God's Word Rightly

I want to again assert the pre-eminence of God's Word. It is our guide for judging others with righteous judgment. Is the person proclaiming the Word of God? Is it biblically true? Accepting the fact that God's Word is both foundational and central, however, is not the only criterion. Satan will quote Scripture. He even had the audacity to quote it to Jesus. Any organization can make up a doctrinal statement. We have even encountered hard-core Satanists who have infiltrated the church and occupied leadership positions in evangelical ministries.

Paul warned:

> For such men are false apostles, deceitful workers, disguising themselves as apostles of Christ. And no wonder, for even Satan disguises himself as an angel of light. Therefore it is not surprising if his servants also disguise themselves as

servants of righteousness; whose end shall be according to their deeds (2 Corinthians 11:13-15).

There is a false teacher in the Southern California area who teaches the Bible. In fact, he teaches the Bible very well but his moral life is decadent. Two of our seminary students were mesmerized by his intellectual brilliance. I personally wouldn't care to do intellectual battle with him, but I wouldn't want to battle Satan either. This man indulges the flesh in its corrupt desires and despises authority, which are traits identified in 2 Peter 2:10 as those of a false prophet.

I'm always amazed at how gullible some people are and how easily deceived. "He's such a wonderful speaker!" "What a charismatic person!" "I could feel the electricity in the air!" They're not judging righteously; they're judging by appearance (or worse, by how they feel). John wrote, "Little children, let no one deceive you; the one who practices righteousness is righteous, just as He is righteous; the one who practices sin is of the devil" (1 John 3:7,8).

Our Guide to Truth

If we know the truth, the lie is obvious. Our focus is not dispelling the darkness, but turning on the light. Our major concern is the righteous leading of the Holy Spirit who will lead us into all truth. The presence of the Holy Spirit in our lives serves as the only foundation for the development of godly character. Notice how truth, righteousness and peace come together in the following three verses:

> Surely His salvation is near to those who fear Him, that glory may dwell in our land. Lovingkindness and truth have met together; righteousness and peace have kissed each other (Psalm 85:9,10).
> The work of righteousness will be peace, and the service of righteousness, quietness and confidence forever (Isaiah 32:17).
> Blessed are those who hunger and thirst for righteousness, for they shall be satisfied (Matthew 5:6).

Christians have frequently relied upon a sense of peace as evidence of the Holy Spirit's leading. It is common to hear people say, "I just don't have a peace about it." I think that is legitimate. I would be concerned about the person who proceeds when his spirit is disturbed. God doesn't lead through anxiety. We are to cast our anxiety upon Jesus, because He cares for us (1 Peter 5:7).

Still, a lot of money is spent on the temporary "cure" of anxiety. People consume alcohol, take illegal drugs, turn to the refrigerator, have sex, mindlessly repeat mantras and escape to cabins, boats and motor homes—all to reduce their anxiety. One lady said, "Whenever I feel anxious, I go on a shopping spree!" Prescription drugs are regularly dispensed for the ails brought on by anxiety.

The bartender, drug pusher, occult practitioner and other peddlers of escapism all have one thing in common: They really don't care about the consumer. They are out to make a profit. Even worse, when the temporary "cure" wears off, we have to return to the same world with the added problem of hangovers and other negative consequences of fake healers.

This "cure" is not new. Nearly 2500 years ago the prophet Jeremiah proclaimed:

> For from the least of them even to the greatest of them, everyone is greedy for gain, and from the prophet even to the priest everyone deals falsely. And they have healed the brokenness of My people superficially saying, "Peace, peace," but there is no peace. Were they ashamed because of the abomination they have done? They were not even ashamed at all; They did not even know how to blush (Jeremiah 6:13-15).

With Truth Comes Peace

Eternally, we have peace with God: "Therefore having been justified by faith, we have peace with God through our Lord Jesus Christ" (Romans 5:1).

Externally, we want peace on earth, but we may not always have that: "If possible, so far as it depends upon you, be at peace with all men" (Romans 12:18). Some things are beyond our right or ability to control. Insecure people often seek peace by ordering their external world. Their peace depends on controlling people and circumstances. There is no person more insecure than a controller.

Let's face it: External peace doesn't always depend upon us. We should always seek to be peacemakers (see Matthew 5:9), but our sense of self-worth cannot be based on an external world that we may or may not be able to control. The fruit of the Spirit is "self-control," not spouse-control or child-control or circumstance-control.

Internally, we desperately need the peace of God:

> Be anxious for nothing, but in everything by prayer and supplication with thanksgiving let your requests be made known to God. And the peace of God, which surpasses all comprehension, shall guard your hearts and your minds in Christ Jesus (Philippians 4:6,7).

The awareness of a troubled spirit should drive us to find the peace of God by turning to Him and assuming our responsibility to use our minds:

> Finally, brethren, whatever is true, whatever is right, whatever is pure, whatever is lovely, whatever is of good repute, if there is any excellence and if anything worthy of praise, let your mind dwell on these things (Philippians 4:8).

We seek the peace of God by ordering our internal world. Consider it like this:

Eternal: - - - - - - Peace *with* God - - - - - What we have

Internal: - - - - - Peace *of* God - - - - - - - What we need

External: - - - - - Peace *on* earth - - - - - - What we want

Resolving Barriers to Peace

To be anxious is to be double-minded, and a double-minded man is unstable in all his ways (James 1:8). I believe there are two tensions in our minds that rob us of God's peace and thus inhibit His guidance in our lives. Both are addressed by Jesus in the Sermon on the Mount (Matthew 6:19-34).

Tension 1: Where Our Treasure Is

The first tension is double-mindedness over treasure or possessions. We're basically in love with what we believe to be our highest good. There are material goods which Jesus identifies as "treasures upon earth." And there are immaterial goods which Jesus calls "treasures in heaven." "Treasures upon earth" have two characteristics. First, all things decay physically. If rust doesn't destroy what we have, then moths or termites will. I had a friend who owned what most Americans only dream of: a cabin in the hills and a boat in the marina. What impressed me was the tremendous amount of energy he expended to keep both in repair. He probably would have experienced a lot more peace if he'd rented a cabin or a boat and let somebody else take care of repairs.

Second, because of the value of earthly treasures, there is always a concern for security. It is hard to be anxiety-free if we are worried about our possessions. The more we possess, the more we cause others to covet. Hence, the reason for "thieves to break in and steal."

On the other hand, "treasures in heaven" are beyond the reach of thieves and secure from the ravages of moths and rust. Paul puts it this way:

> On the other hand discipline yourself for the purpose of Godliness. For bodily discipline is only of little profit, but Godliness is profitable for all things, for it holds promise for the present life and for the life to come (1 Timothy 4:7,8).

People seem to want the best of both worlds. But if we concentrate on treasures in this one, we will miss out on treasures in the next. If we store our treasures in the next life, God may throw in extra blessing in this one. Jesus states it plainly:

> Do not lay up for yourselves treasures upon earth, but lay up for yourselves treasures in heaven. For where your treasure is, there will your heart be also (Matthew 6:19).

Question! What do you treasure in your heart? What would you exchange for love, joy, peace, patience, kindness, goodness, faithfulness, gentleness and self-control? Would you exchange those for a new car, a cabin in the hills, a boat in the marina, exceptional status at the top of the corporate ladder? Jesus reminded the crowd, "Beware, and be on guard against every form of greed; for not even when one has an abundance does his life consist of his possessions" (Luke 12:15).

A man's life consists of who he serves. There is a moral healthiness and simple, unaffected goodness present in the single-minded person that is absent from the one serving many masters. Jesus said:

> No one can serve two masters. For either he will hate the one and love the other, or he will hold to one and despise the other. You cannot serve God and mammon. For this reason I say to you, do not be anxious (Matthew 6:24,25).

There will be no peace serving two masters. To whichever master we yield, by that master we shall be controlled.

Tension 2: Double-mindedness Over Tomorrow

The second tension is double-mindedness over tomorrow. The first tension dealt with possessions. This one deals with provision. The materialist struggles with the first tension; the doubter struggles with the second.

The question is, can we trust God? Jesus answered by saying:

> Look at the birds of the air, they do not sow, neither do they reap, nor gather into barns, and yet your heavenly Father feeds them. Are you not worth much more than they? (Matthew 6:26)

Trusting God for tomorrow is a question of our worth. Birds are not created in the image of God. We are! Birds will not inherit the kingdom of God, but we shall. Birds are mortal; mankind is immortal. If God takes care of the birds, so much more will He take care of us. That's why the apostle Paul could write, "My God shall supply all your needs according to His riches in glory in Christ Jesus" (Philippians 4:19).

Observe the lilies of the field:

> If God so arrays the grass of the field, which is alive today and tomorrow is thrown into the furnace, will He not do much more for you O men of little faith? Do not be anxious then! (Matthew 6:30,31)

God lays His own reputation on the line. If we trust and obey, He will provide. This is a question of God's integrity.

> For God knows we have need of all these things. . . .
> Therefore do not be anxious for tomorrow; for tomorrow will
> care for itself. Each day has enough trouble of its own (Matthew
> 6:32,34).

The essential will of God is that we live responsibly today and trust Him for tomorrow. Are we people of little faith, or do we really believe that the fruit of the Spirit will satisfy us more than earthly possessions? Do we really believe that if we hunger and thirst after righteousness, we shall be satisfied? Do we really believe that if we seek to establish God's kingdom, God will supply all our needs according to His riches in glory? If we do, then we will "seek first His kingdom and His righteousness, and all these things shall be added to you" (Matthew 6:33).

Limiting Anxious Feelings

Let's assume your first priority is the kingdom of God, and you deeply believe that God and His righteousness will satisfy. You have sought God's will for a certain direction, and you believe that He has led you to make specific plans. The problem is, you are still worried about whether your plans will come about as you had hoped. That's okay. I believe a little anxiety is needed to motivate us to responsible behavior. When I'm facing such situations, I try to follow the six steps described below to limit my anxious feelings. They have been summarized in an "Anxiety Worksheet" at the end of the chapter.

First, *state the problem.* A problem well-stated is half-solved. In anxious states of mind, people can't see the forest for the trees. Put the problem in perspective. Will it matter for eternity? Generally speaking, the process of worrying takes a greater toll on a person than the negative consequences of what they are worrying about. I've had a lot of anxious people come into my office who only need their problem clarified.

The danger at this juncture is to seek ungodly counsel. The world is glutted with magicians and sorcerers who will promise incredible results. Their appearance may be striking. Their credentials may be impressive. Their personality may be charming. But their character is bankrupt. "Judge righteously not according to appearance," Jesus said (John 7:24). "How blessed is the man who does not walk in the counsel of the wicked, nor stand in the path of sinners, nor sit in the seat of scoffers" (Psalm 1:1).

Second, *divide the facts from the assumptions.* People may be fearful of the facts, but not anxious. We're anxious because we don't know what's going to happen tomorrow. Since we don't know, we make assumptions. A peculiar trait of the mind is its tendency to assume the worst. If the assumption is accepted as truth, it will drive the mind to its anxiety limits. If you act upon the assumption, you will be counted among the fools! Therefore, as best as possible, separate the assumptions from the facts.

Third, *determine what you have the right or ability to control.* You are responsible for that which you can control, and you are not responsible for that which you can't. Your self-worth is tied only to that for which you are responsible. If you aren't living a responsible life, you should feel anxious! Don't try to cast your responsibility onto Christ; He will throw it back. But do cast your anxiety onto Him. His integrity is at stake in meeting your needs if you are living a responsible life.

Fourth, *list everything you can do which is related to the situation that is under your responsibility.* When people don't assume their responsibility, they turn to temporary cures for their anxiety. Remember, "The work of righteousness will be peace" (Isaiah 32:17). Turning to an unrighteous solution will only increase anxiety in the future.

Fifth, *once you are sure you have fulfilled your responsibility, see if there is any way you can help others.* Turning your attention away from your own self-absorption and onto helping people around you is not only the loving thing to do, but it also brings a special inner peace that comes from knowing you have helped someone in need.

Sixth, *the rest is God's responsibility,* except for your prayer, according to Philippians 4:6-8. Any residual anxiety is probably due to assuming responsibilities that God never intended you to have.

A friend of mine called after several months of sleepless nights and anxious days. She had served the Lord through a missions organization for many years. A philosophical difference resulted in a parting of the ways. Declining health resulted in much physical pain. Her list of doctors was endless. Now she was asking me if seeing a secular counselor who specializes in hypnosis for pain reduction was advisable. I expressed my reservations and asked if we could get together. I suspected a little spiritual pride kept her from seeking the help of Christian friends for counsel.

After a couple of hours resolving spiritual conflicts, she found her peace with God. Her entire countenance changed and she said on her way out, "I feel like I have been set free!"

"You have," I responded. The peace of God that passes all understanding was now guarding her mind.

What a priceless commodity is the peace that results from judging rightly the influences that invade our lives. And to think that God gives us His Word and His Spirit so that we can know the truth and receive His calm. Would you join me in this prayer to receive His peace?

Dear Heavenly Father, I desire Your peace. I therefore commit myself to live a righteous life. Forgive me for seeking treasures on earth instead of treasures in heaven. I thank You for the possessions You have entrusted to me in this life, but I choose to believe that my life does not consist of my possessions. My life is in Christ, and I want the fruit of the Spirit to be evident in me so that I may glorify You.

I bring my anxious thoughts before You concerning Your provision for tomorrow. I choose to trust You by seeking first Your kingdom and Your righteousness. I know that all other things will be added to me, and I trust You to meet my needs. I commit myself to order my internal world around You. Forgive me for the times I have tried to control people and circumstances that I had no right or ability to control. I cast my anxiety upon You and commit myself to be responsible today for what You have entrusted with me. Amen.

Anxiety Worksheet

1. State the problem.

2. Divide the facts from the assumptions.
   a. Identify the facts relating to the situation.
   b. Identify the assumptions relating to the situation.
   c. Verify the assumptions.

3. Determine what you have the right or ability to control.
   a. What you can control as a matter of personal responsibility.
   b. What you cannot or should not control.

4. List everything related to the situation that is your responsibility.

5. If you have fulfilled your responsibility, how can you help others?

6. The rest is God's responsibility, except for prayer, according to Philippians 4:6.

*How does God work through
human responsibility to bring
about His will?*

10

SANCTIFIED COMMON SENSE

Have you heard about the devout Christian who heard an urgent news report on his radio that a flash flood was within minutes of entering the peaceful valley where he lived? Immediately he went to his knees and committed his life to the Lord and prayed for safety. The words were still on his lips when he became aware that water was gushing under his door. He retreated to the second floor and finally onto the roof of his house.

While he sat on the roof, a helicopter flew by and the pilot asked over the loudspeaker if they could lift him off. "It's not necessary since I have the Lord's protection," he replied.

Moments later the house began to break up and he found himself clinging to a tree. A police boat, braving the waters, approached him for rescue, but he assured them that the Lord would save him. Finally, the tree gave way and the man went to his death.

Standing before the Lord, he asked, "Lord, I'm glad to be here, but why didn't you answer my prayer for safety?" The Lord responded, "Son, I told you over the radio to get out of there. Then I sent you a helicopter and a motor boat!"

Nowhere in the Bible are we given the idea that God works only in the extraordinary. Much of the time He supernaturally works through His created order. Many people think God is present only when there is a miracle and that He leads only through signs and wonders.

This kind of mindset is seen in John 7:25-27. The Jewish people were commenting about Jesus: "Is this not the man whom they are seeking to kill? Look, He is speaking in public. The rulers do not really know that this is the Christ, do they? However, we know where this man is from; but whenever the Christ may come, no one knows where He is from."

They were looking for a mystery man, seeking a sign when the real signs of Jesus' divine character and fulfillment of Scripture were there all the time.

Looking for signs is understandable. There is always some anxiety concerning the decision we have made or are about to make. Naturally, we want to make the right decision and be in God's will, so there is the temptation to ask for some sign of confirmation from God.

Then there are those people who *always* look for a sign. They walk by sight, not by faith. To them, God is present only in the miraculous. God was "really" at the church service if something unusual happened. Many desire and look for "visitations" from God.

But how does that square with God's omnipresence and the fact that He will never leave nor forsake us? Isn't God at every church service? Since God created the fixed order of the universe, would you expect Him to work primarily within that fixed order or outside of it? If God gave us an instruction manual, shouldn't we expect Him to operate within the confinements of it? If God gave us a watch, would we be honoring Him more by asking what time it is, or by simply consulting the watch?

God's Way

I believe in miracles, and I accept as fact every one recorded in the Bible. I believe that our entire Christian experience is a miracle. It simply cannot be explained by natural means. And God's power is seen in other miraculous ways today, but must He always prove Himself by stepping outside His created order? If God doesn't primarily guide us through His Word (which never changes) and take into account the fixed order of the universe, how can we ever have any stability? How can we make any plans if God doesn't reveal His ways and then stay consistent with them?

I challenge you to take an exhaustive concordance and look up every reference for "way" and "ways." You will find that God is not capricious in His dealings with man. He has clearly established ways and He is faithful to them. Let me illustrate with just a few references:

> I pray Thee, if I have found favor in Thy sight, let me know Thy ways, that I may know Thee (Exodus 33:13).
> Therefore, you shall keep the commandments of the Lord your God, to walk in His ways and to fear Him (Deuteronomy 8:6).

Moving to the New Testament, we see John the Baptist storming on the scene announcing, "Make ready the way of the Lord" (Mark 1:3). And Jesus said, "I am the way" (John 14:6).

I believe God has revealed His ways, and we are to walk in them. The question is, how does God work through human responsibility and the natural order of the universe to bring about His will? Somehow He works through a less-than-perfect church, orchestrating human affairs in such a way as to guarantee the outcome of the ages. What really impresses me is His timing, not His miraculous interventions.

Notice how Jesus responded to those who insisted on a sign:

> Then some of the scribes and Pharisees answered Him saying, "Teacher, we want a sign from You." But He answered and said to them, "An evil and adulterous generation craves for a sign; and yet no sign shall be given to it but the sign of Jonah the prophet" (Matthew 12:38,39).

Satan wanted a sign too. He said, "If You are the Son of God, throw Yourself down" (Matthew 4:6). To this Jesus responded, "You shall not put the Lord your God to the test" (Matthew 4:7). Jesus was saying that the sign we need is the Word of God, and we are to use the Word to guard against Satan's temptations to force the Lord to prove Himself.

What About Signs and Wonders?

Signs and wonders validated the ministry of Jesus and the apostles. After quoting from the prophet Joel and demonstrating that the outpouring of the Spirit at Pentecost was biblical, Peter preached:

> Men of Israel, listen to these words: Jesus the Nazarene, a man attested to you by God with miracles and wonders and signs which God performed through Him in your midst, just as you yourselves know (Acts 2:22).

Of the apostles, Paul said, "The signs of a true apostle were performed among you with all perseverance, by signs and wonders and miracles" (2 Corinthians 12:12).

However, signs and wonders would also accompany false teachers and false prophets (Matthew 7:21-23; 2 Peter 2:1-22). In fact, biblical references to signs and wonders in the last days are nearly all credited to false teachers, false prophets and false Christs (Matthew 24:11,24). The false prophet in the tribulation will perform great signs, "and he deceives those who dwell on the earth because of the signs which it was given to him to perform" (Revelation 13:14).

Jesus is no longer with us in the flesh, and there are no more apostles. Jesus identified the sign of a disciple as markedly different: "By this all men will know that you are My disciples, if you have love for one another" (John 13:35).

Does this mean that signs and wonders have ceased? I certainly don't want to be identified with an evil generation that seeks a sign, but I also don't want to be associated with the powerless anti-supernaturalism evidenced in Western rationalism. Both the power of God and the wisdom of God are expressed in Christ. Paul said,

> For indeed Jews ask for a sign, and Greeks search for wisdom; but we preach Christ crucified, to Jews a stumbling block, and to Gentiles foolishness, but to those who are the called, both Jews and Greeks, Christ the power of God and the wisdom of God (1 Corinthians 1:22-24).

The Wisdom of God

Wisdom was certainly the way of the Old Testament as the book of Proverbs and other wisdom literature attest. However, in the Old Testament, wisdom was not understood as our ability to reason independent of God. Rather, it was an acceptance and knowledge of divine revelation. Biblical wisdom is seeing life from God's perspective. In contrast, Western world rationalism is interpreting life from man's perspective. When wisdom degenerates to rationalism, our walk with God is reduced to an intellectual pursuit rather than a living relationship. Proverbs 3:5-7 pictures the relationship God desires with us:

> Trust in the Lord with all your heart, and do not lean on your own understanding. In all your ways acknowledge Him, and He will make your paths straight. Do not be wise in your own eyes; Fear the Lord and turn away from evil.

Turning away from evil signifies that there are moral boundaries. Some believe that the will of God is to live inside of those boundaries. They think that if we are morally right with God, He has no fixed plan for our lives. We are free to live as we please as long as we stay morally pure and exercise biblical wisdom. Since all unbelievers are outside the moral boundaries of God, they can expect judgment. Christians living outside the moral boundaries can expect discipline. The writer of Hebrews would attest to the latter: "But if you are without discipline, of which all have become partakers, then you are illegitimate children and not sons" (Hebrews 12:8).

It's true that God does give us freedom to make choices on non-moral issues, but He expects us to know His Word and make wise decisions. He has made His will known primarily in His Word, and He delights when we humbly submit to it and obey. But we are not Old Testament saints. We are New Testament Christians. Christ has reconciled Jew and Gentile, and we possess both power and wisdom. What marks the church age is that we now have the presence of the Holy Spirit who will guide us into all truth.

For the rest of this chapter, we'll look at seven ways in which we commonly seek God's guidance and conclude with ten factors that will help lead you toward a wise decision. Much of this book deals with God's presence, both counterfeit and true. His presence brings conviction when I'm out of His will and a peace when I'm in it. The Holy Spirit enables us to discern when we're being influenced by a counterfeit spirit.

Seven Common Methods of Seeking God's Guidance

1. Conscience

Folklore advises, "Let your conscience be your guide." This has serious limitations since our conscience is a function of our mind. Having been conformed to this world, it can be programmed wrongly. A conscience is always true to its own standard. Until we come to Christ, the standard is the world system we were raised in. Many people are falsely guided by a guilty conscience—not a true guilt, but a psychological guilt usually developed in early childhood. Satan works through this stronghold to accuse the brethren day and night (Revelation 12:10).

People like this are usually perfectionists who labor under condemnation, even though the Bible says, "There is no condemnation for those who are in Christ Jesus" (Romans 8:1). They aren't led; they are driven. They constantly look for affirmation. They have a tendency to be man-pleasers. Paul said, "If I were still striving to please men, I would not be a bond-servant of Christ" (Galatians 1:10). If you are striving to please men, who are you a bond-servant of?

Since our minds were conformed to this world we need to renew them in such a way that what we believe is in accordance to truth. Chapter 14 of Romans is dealing with how we should walk in regard to non-moral issues. Paul says,

> The faith which you have, have as your own conviction before God. Happy is he who does not condemn himself in what he approves. But he who doubts is condemned (Romans 14:22,23).

In other words, be very cautious about going against your own conscience once you are committed to Christ. The Holy

Spirit does work through our conscience as He seeks to renew our minds. However, we are to restrict our freedom if it causes a weaker brother to stumble. We never have the right to violate another person's conscience. Paul says, "I also do my best to maintain always a blameless conscience both before God and before men" (Acts 24:16).

2. Fleeces

"If the sun is shining in the morning, I'll do it."

"If he's there when I open the door, I'll know he's the one."

"If I pass the class on world missions, I'll be a missionary. If not, I'll be a local pastor."

We all know better than this, but it's amazing how often scenarios just like these pop into our heads. We refer to such propositions as laying a "fleece" before the Lord. The term *fleece* comes from the account of Gideon.

In Judges 6, Gideon is called by God to deliver Israel from the Mideonites. Gideon questions whether God is even for Israel (6:13), and he doubts his own ability (6:15). So he asks God for a sign (6:17). God gives him one, then tells him to take the family ox and tear down the altar of Baal. Gideon is afraid to go during the day, so he goes at night. Then he questions again whether God will deliver Israel. This time he puts a lamb's fleece on the ground. If God will deliver, then the lamb's fleece will be wet in the morning and the ground around it will be dry. The next morning it is so. That ought to satisfy him, right?

Wrong! Wanting to be sure, and hoping that God won't get too mad, Gideon asks Him to do it again, but this time with the opposite results (i.e., the fleece dry and the ground wet). Not exactly the stuff heroes are made of. But God answers Gideon's request and then He reduces Gideon's army down to 300 men!

The whole point of the passage is that God, not man, is the deliverer. God chose a man desperately seeking assurance and reduced an army down to nothing so that the victory would clearly be His. The fleece wasn't a means of demonstrating faith; it was just the opposite. And it certainly wasn't used to determine God's will. God had already told Gideon what to do. Gideon was questioning the integrity of God, just as we do if we ask for a fleece when God has already shown us His will.

3. Circumstances

Some of us tend to assume that it is God's will if the circumstances are favorable and it isn't God's will if the circumstances are unfavorable. Next to the Bible, I would guess that more Christians are "guided" by this means than any other. Yet of all the possible means of guidance, this is the least authoritative and trustworthy.

As I mentioned before, I had the privilege of pastoring a church that purchased new property and went through a building program. Through most of the process the circumstances didn't seem favorable. Twice I sat with the mayor, who was also a local realtor, and asked him if he thought our plans were feasible. He advised us not to make the land trade, and he didn't think the city would allow us to build. He knew the real estate and the political climate better than anyone in the city.

But even the advice of experts didn't prove reliable. The land swap increased our assets by millions and the city planning commission voted 7-0 in favor of our building plans. You may have to set sail by the tide, but you'd better be guided by the stars or you're going to end up on the wrong shore. Circumstances may have their effect on your plans, but you have a far greater accountability to God. Make sure you follow Him, not the tide of circumstance.

I heard a motivational speaker say, "I don't like to recruit Christians because when the going gets tough they quit, concluding that it must not be God's will." Generally speaking, I believe that Christians should live above life's circumstances and not be guided by them. Establishing God's kingdom on earth is going to be an uphill fight. But Paul says, "I have learned to be content in whatever circumstance I am" (Philippians 4:11).

Also, be careful about applying too much significance to unusual circumstances or coincidences. "It must be God's will. Why else would that book be lying there!" It could be God's will, but I would never take that kind of sign on its own merit. If, for example, you keep coming across another person's path, maybe you should check it out. If it is more than a coincidence, you will quickly find out when you talk with the person.

I have counseled too many people in occultic bondage who have made bizarre associations or attached far too much significance to irrelevant events.

4. Godly Counsel

Proverbs 11:14 says, "Where there is no guidance, the people fall, but in abundance of counselors there is victory." The reason for this is obvious. No one person has complete knowledge, and everyone has a limited perspective on the truth. God has structured the church in such a way that we need each other. I have made some dumb decisions that would never have been made if I had consulted someone. However, some people will only consult those who agree with them. That's a sign of immaturity.

At the same time, the counsel of others does have to be weighed. There is a fascinating account in Acts 21 where the Holy Spirit seemed to be warning Paul not to go to Jerusalem. Disciples in Tyre "kept telling Paul through the Spirit not to set foot in Jerusalem" (21:4). Then a prophet named Agabus gave a visual demonstration by binding himself and saying, "This is what the Holy Spirit says: 'In this way the Jews at Jerusalem will bind the man who owns this belt [Paul] and deliver him into the hands of the Gentiles' " (21:11). Everyone began begging him not to go. Paul responded:

"What are you doing, weeping and breaking my heart? For I am ready not only to be bound, but even die at Jerusalem for the name of the Lord Jesus." And since he would not be persuaded, we fell silent, remarking, "The will of the Lord be done!" (Acts 21:13,14)

Was the Holy Spirit guiding the disciples and Agabus? The information was mostly true, but the conclusion of the disciples wasn't. The Holy Spirit wasn't trying to prevent Paul from going; He was preparing Paul for coming persecution. Paul was right in not wanting to take the easy way out.

The missionary Hudson Taylor went against advice, and circumstances nearly destroyed him. But he, more than anyone, opened up China to the gospel. Sometimes people can tell you the truth, but they draw selfish conclusions. Sometimes we need to ascertain our own motives as well as those of the people we seek counsel from, for our motives can be in error as well. The value of counsel is to get an unbiased opinion from a spiritually sensitive person which you can add to the recipe of ingredients God is giving to guide you.

5. Gifts and Abilities

After I taught a class on spiritual gifts, a young man came to me and asked, "Is my gift prophecy or exhortation?" Knowing him very well, I was careful as I responded. "I don't think either one is your gift," I began. "But if I have ever known someone who has the gift of helps, you're it. You're sensitive to the needs of other people and always ready to help."

A look of disappointment came over his face. "I knew it!" he responded. Struggling with a low self-esteem, he was pursuing what he wrongly perceived to be a greater gift.

God hasn't distributed gifts and talents equally, and for that reason alone we can be assured that our sense of self-worth isn't to be based on what we do. Our self-acceptance comes from our identity in Christ and our growth in character. Show me someone who understands who he is as a child of God and whose character exemplifies the fruit of the Spirit, and I will show you someone with a healthy self-image.

Every child of God has the same identity and opportunity to grow. Only when our identity is firmly established and we have matured to the point where the fruit of the Spirit is evident will we use our gifts and talents to edify others.

God has known us from the foundation of the world. He has entrusted us with certain life endowments. He will certainly lead us in a way that makes use of our gifts and talents. It is our responsibility to take advantage of every opportunity as it arrives. Tragically, many people go to the grave with their music still in them, never contributing to the symphony of God's work. They never realize their potential nor take the risks that faith requires. They hang onto the security of the tree trunk, but the fruit is always on the endof the limb.

6. Duty

Do you know how much of our Christian calling is simply a matter of duty? Most of it. You don't need God to tell you to live a responsible life. He already has. You don't need some subjective confirmation for every decision.

I confess that I don't "feel led" to do a lot of things. There are mornings I don't feel like getting out of bed. And I have never felt led to visit a convalescent hospital. The smell inside the front door has never confirmed my "leading" to be there. I have left feeling blessed, however, experiencing the truth of what Jesus said: "If you know these things, you are blessed if you do them" (John 13:17).

7. Desires

The psalmist wrote, "Delight yourself in the Lord; and He will give you the desires of your heart" (Psalm 37:4). The key is to delight yourself in the Lord. If you do, your desires will change. I believe this process unfolds as we seek to do God's will.

I had very little desire to read until I came to Christ. Now I read volumes. After I received Christ, I wanted to serve Him full time. I had completed engineering school and was prepared to do anything God wanted, except go back to school. Within a year I could hardly wait to get to seminary. It was the best educational experience of my life, and the only one I enjoyed up to that point. Since then I have finished four more degrees. I never had a desire to write a book until three years ago, and this is my third one. If we delight ourselves in the Lord, He does change our desires!

We struggle between the desires of the flesh and the desires of righteousness. Jesus told us, "Blessed are those who hunger and thirst for righteousness, for they shall be satisfied" (Matthew 5:6). Do you believe that? I guarantee that if you try to satisfy the desires of the flesh, you will never satisfy them. The more you feed them, the greater the hunger.

When we first come to Christ, nothing contests our will more than the lusts of the flesh: "For the flesh set its desire against the Spirit, and Spirit against the flesh; for these are in opposition to one another" (Galatians 5:17). Our will is like a toggle switch, but it's initially spring-loaded to the flesh. In a mature Christian, it's spring-loaded to the Spirit. In determining God's will for your life, do you intend to satisfy the flesh or the Spirit?

Ten Factors Leading to a Wise Decision

At the end of the chapter you will find a checklist titled, "Ten Deciding Factors." These are ten questions you'll want to ask yourself and pray about when you're faced with a decision. The first five are generic. They represent moral issues and godly wisdom that are normative for all times. The next five are questions that you need to ask when facing a change in direction. Let's take a look at what each question entails.

First, *have you prayed about it?* The Lord's Prayer begins with a petition for His will. Prayer was never intended to be a fourth-down punting situation in which we ask God to bail us out of our hasty decisions. It was intended to be a first-down huddle. We aren't supposed to ask God to bless our plans; we're supposed to ask God for His plans.

God could just give us what we need, but He taught us to pray, "Give us this day our daily bread." Nothing establishes dependency more than prayer. Dependency puts us in a right position with God since the flesh operates independently of God. The tendency is to try everything but God first and then when that fails say, "Well I guess there is nothing else to do now but to pray." But we are to "seek first His Kingdom and His righteousness."

Second, *is it consistent with the Word of God?* In our culture, ignorance is no excuse since resources abound. I believe that every home should have at least a concordance, Bible dictionary, topical Bible, a good commentary and a study Bible with notes. Most communities in America have a pastor within driving distance or one who is reachable by phone. Most pastors would love to share what God has to say about a given matter. If they wouldn't, you have called the wrong pastor!

We also have an abundance of radio programs with great messages, and some even invite people to call in with questions. Christian literature discusses every imaginable problem. You can receive valuable input to help you make a decision if you will make a habit of consulting the Bible and godly resources.

Third, *can I do it and be a positive Christian witness?* Asking that question years ago prompted me to give up bridge and golf. Now that I have matured a little, I can play them again!

A seminary student stopped by my office and told me about a job he had been offered. It would take care of his financial needs, but he had some reservations concerning the sales pitch he was required to use. I asked him if he could use the sales technique and be a positive witness for Christ. He didn't take the job.

This simple question will govern a lot of behavior. Several spin-off questions are helpful: Would I do that if Jesus were here? Would I go to that movie if Jesus were my escort? Can I tell that joke from the pulpit?

Fourth, *will the Lord be glorified?* Can I do this and give glory to God? In doing it, would I be glorifying God in my body? Am I seeking the glory of man or glory of God? Am I doing this to be noticed by man or am I seeking to please the Lord? Driven people will do it just to get the approval of others. Those sent by God seek His glory.

Fifth, *am I acting responsibly?* God doesn't bail us out of our irresponsibility. He will let us suffer the consequences of our sins and irresponsible choices. But when we are faithful in little things, he will put us in charge of greater things. Don't get ahead of God's timing or you will be over your head in responsibilities. Seek to develop your life and message, and God will expand your ministry.

Sixth, *is it reasonable?* God expects us to think. His guidance may transcend human reasoning, but it never excludes it. God doesn't bypass our mind; He operates through it: "Brethren, do not be children in your thinking; yet in evil be babes, but in your thinking be mature" (1 Corinthians 14:20). We are warned in Scripture not to put our mind in neutral. We are to think and practice what we know to be true (Philippians 4:8,9).

Seventh, *does a realistic opportunity exist?* Closed doors are not meant to be knocked down. If you have a hopeless scheme, let it go. If it isn't God's timing, wait. If a realistic opportunity exists, and all the other factors are in agreement, then take the plunge. God may open a window of opportunity, but it will close if not taken advantage of. The faithless man asks, "What do I stand to lose if I do?" The faithful man asks, "What do I risk losing if I don't?"

Eighth, *are unbiased, spiritually sensitive associates in agreement?* Be careful not to consult only those who will agree with you. Give your advisors permission to ask hard questions. Don't be afraid of no answers. If it isn't God's will, don't you want to know before you make the mistake of acting impulsively?

Ninth, *do I have a sanctified desire?* Don't think that being in the will of God must always be an unpleasant task. The joy of the Lord should be our strength. I find my greatest joy in serving God and being in His will. But don't get the idea that if everything is wonderful you must be in the will of God. Is this a desire to satisfy a lust of the flesh, or a Spirit-filled desire to see God's kingdom established and people helped?

Tenth, *do I have a peace about it?* This is an inner peace. In the world you will have tribulation, but in Christ we have the assurance of overcoming the world. Is the peace of God guarding your heart and your mind?

If you have been able to answer yes to all ten of these deciding factors, what are you waiting for?

I'm not sure who the author is, but Kyle Rote, Jr., shared the following article at a Fellowship of Christian Athletes gathering:

> I am part of the "Fellowship of the Unashamed." I have Holy Spirit Power. The dye has been cast. I've stepped over the line. The decision has been made. I am a disciple of His. I won't look back, let up, slow down, back away or be still. My past is redeemed, my present makes sense and my future is secure. I am finished and done with low living, sight walking, small planning, smooth knees, colorless dreams, tame visions, mundane talking, chincy giving and dwarfed goals!
>
> I no longer need pre-eminence, prosperity, position, promotions, plaudits or popularity. I don't have to be right, first, tops, recognized, praised, regarded or rewarded. I now live by presence, lean by faith, love by patience, lift by prayer and labor by power.
>
> My face is set, my gait is fast, my goal is heaven, my road is narrow, my way is rough, my companions few, my guide reliable, my mission clear. I cannot be bought, compromised,

detoured, lured away, turned back, diluted or delayed. I will not flinch in the face of sacrifice, hesitate in the presence of adversity, negotiate at the table of the enemy, ponder at the pool of popularity or meander in the maze of mediocrity.

I won't give up, shut up, let up or burn up till I've preached up, prayed up, paid up, stored up and stayed up for the cause of Christ.

I am a disciple of Jesus. I must go till He comes, give till I drop, preach till all know and work till He stops.

And when He comes to get His own, He'll have no problems recognizing me. My colors will be clear.

We have seen that God's ways are established. He has spoken through His Word and He already is working in our lives. The question is whether we see and seek His direction or are influenced by false guides. If you would like to tell God of your desire to find and follow His will for your life in ways that honor Him, then would you pray with me?

D ear Lord, I thank You that I do not have to drift through life in uncertainty, never really being sure that my steps are being guided by You. I thank You that I can have the privilege of walking according to Your way.

Lord, keep me from looking for signs when You have already spoken so clearly in Your Word. And don't let me be bound by circumstances, but help me seek the wisdom that is from above through Your Word and the godly counsel of others.

I again commit myself to desiring Your will, Your glory and the fruit that will result in my life and others as I walk with You. Thank You, Lord. I know the way will not always be easy, but it will be the path of joy and peace. Amen.

Ten Deciding Factors

	Yes	No
For all decisions		
1. Have I prayed about it?	❑	❑
2. Is it consistent with the Word of God?	❑	❑
3. Can I have a positive Christian witness?	❑	❑
4. Will the Lord be glorified?	❑	❑
5. Am I acting responsibly?	❑	❑

Direction-changing decisions

6. Is it reasonable?   ❑   ❑

    What makes sense?

    What doesn't make sense?

7. Does a realistic opportunity exist?   ❑   ❑

    Factors for:

    Factors against:

8. Are unbiased, spiritually sensitive people
   in agreement?   ❑   ❑

    Those for:

    Those against:

9. Do I have a sanctified desire?   ❑   ❑

    Why?

    Why not?

10. Do I have a peace about it?   ❑   ❑

    Why?

    Why not?

THE LIFE OF FAITH

After Sunday school one morning, a mother asked her little girl what she had learned. The daughter responded, "I learned how Moses built this pontoon bridge across the Red Sea, and how all these people were transported across with tanks and half-tracks. As soon as they were across, the bridge was blown up just as the Egyptians were coming across and they were all drowned in the Red Sea."

The mother was astonished and asked if that's what the teacher had told her. "Oh no," the little girl replied, "but you would never believe what she really said."

That little girl is like a lot of people. They think that faith is believing what isn't true. And for others, faith is little more than wishful thinking.

After Jesus claimed to be sent by God, some were seeking to seize Him, having come to the conclusion that He was not a good man. But others did believe in Him, "and they were saying, 'When the Christ shall come, He will not perform more signs than those which this man has, will He?' " (John 7:31) All the evidence was there. Some chose to believe; others chose not to. People do the same today. Yet to live within the will of God, you have to believe in the Lord Jesus Christ.

Faith is the operating principle of life. It is the means by which we relate to God and carry out His kingdom activity. Just think of the many ways faith must be operative in our lives.

> For by grace you have been saved through faith; and that not of yourselves, it is the gift of God; not as a result of works, that no one should boast (Ephesians 2:8,9).

We're not only saved by faith, but we also "walk by faith, and not by sight" (2 Corinthians 5:7).

Being found faithful is a prerequisite for ministry: "I thank Christ Jesus our Lord, who has strengthened me, because He considered me faithful, putting me into service" (1 Timothy 1:12). Paul then adds: "And the things which you have heard from me in the presence of many witnesses, these entrust to faithful men, who will be able to teach others also" (2 Timothy 2:2). This is more than being reliable, since a person could be counted on to follow through on an assignment and not be a believer. The added ingredient in faithful people is that they know the truth and can be counted on to be reliable.

Really, the quality of any relationship is determined by faith or trust: "Many a man proclaims his own loyalty, but who can find a trustworthy man?" (Proverbs 20:6) The words *faith, trust* and *believe* are all the same word (*pistis*) in the original language. The man who has faith believes in something. The one who believes also trusts, or he doesn't truly believe. There is no concept that looms larger in life than faith because what we believe determines how we live.

Let's look at three standards of faith which will keep us on the right path if understood and practiced.

1. Faith Is Dependent Upon Its Object

The question is not whether we walk by faith, but what or whom we believe. Everybody walks by faith; it is the operating principle of life. For instance, we drive our cars by faith. When we observe a green traffic light, we don't slow down or stop—we drive right through the intersection. We believe drivers coming from the other direction will see a red light and stop. We never see the red light, but we believe they do. Suppose you didn't believe that. How would you approach the intersection?

When I was a little boy, I popped a dime in a soft drink machine and out came a bottle of pop. (Remember those days?) Without looking, I quickly took a swig of the soda, but immediately spit it out. Then I noticed that the bottom of the bottle was completely filled with junk. I never drank that brand again. Now we drink sodas out of cans by faith! We can't even see what's in the can, but we believe the manufacturer put in the can what the label says.

We already have some beliefs about the world we live in. Whatever we think will make us happy, satisfied or successful is what constitutes our belief system. We are walking by faith according to what we already believe. Be assured that the world system we were raised in didn't establish a biblical belief system in our minds. Because we came into this world separated from God, we learned to live our lives independently from Him. We were conformed to this world. Unless we were raised in a perfect Christian home, much of what we learned to believe didn't reflect biblical truth.

If you believe that you will only be satisfied by owning things, then you will probably never be satisfied. If you believe you are successful because of the amount of toys you accumulate, you will certainly be at odds with Scripture. And if the world system hasn't distorted our faith enough, the New Age movement has given it several new twists. The New Ager operates under the principle that if you believe hard enough, anything will become true. But believing doesn't make it true, and not believing doesn't make it not true. Not believing in hell, for example, doesn't drop the temperature down there one degree!

We don't create reality with our minds. We are incapable of creating anything. We can creatively shove around and rearrange what God has already created, but we are not gods.

To think that we will get what we want if we believe with all our hearts is a faith based on selfish desires. It originates within ourselves and depends on our own ability to believe. It's a form of religious self-hypnosis. It's like the Christian who says, "I don't know the Bible, but I have faith." For that person, faith is a substitute for knowledge and a compensation for ignorance.

The Visible Versus the Invisible

Hope is not wishful thinking: "Now faith is the assurance of things hoped for, the conviction of things not seen" (Hebrews 11:1). Hope is the present assurance of some future good. Biblical faith is not a preference for what we would like to see, but a conviction that what is unseen is real. Biblical faith enables us to see the reality of the spiritual world we presently live in, and we have the assurance of heaven. Only with that kind of faith can we say with Paul, "For I consider the sufferings of this present time are not worthy to be compared with the glory that is to be revealed to us" (Romans 8:18).

According to Scripture, the invisible world is more real than the visible world: "By faith we understand that the worlds were prepared by the word of God, so that what is seen was not made out of the things which are visible" (Hebrews 11:3). The ultimate reality is spiritual, not physical. God is a spirit. Every physical thing we see is only temporal and passing away:

> While we look not at the things which are seen, but at the things which are not seen; for the things which are seen are temporal, but the things which are not seen are eternal (2 Corinthians 4:18).

When Jesus appeared to the frightened band of disciples after His resurrection, He showed them both His hands and His side. Later the disciples informed Thomas of what they had seen, but he responded, "Unless I shall see in His hands the imprint of the nails, and put my finger into the place of the nails, and put my hand into His side, I will not believe" (John 20:25). Thomas was determined to walk by sight, not by faith. The only thing that was real to Thomas was what he could see. Eight days later Jesus appeared again, and said to Thomas:

> "Reach here your finger, and see My hands; and reach here your hand, and put it into My side; and be not unbelieving, but believing." Thomas answered and said to Him, "My Lord and my God!" Jesus said to him, "Because you have seen Me, have you believed? Blessed are they who did not see, and yet believed" (John 20:27-29).

The Object Worthy of Genuine Faith

Scripture asserts that Jesus is the author and perfecter of our faith (Hebrews 12:2). He is the ultimate faith object because He never changes; He is immutable:

> Remember those who led you, who spoke the word of God to you; and considering the result of their conduct, imitate their faith. Jesus Christ is the same yesterday and today, yes and forever (Hebrews 13:7,8).

The sun is perhaps the most credible object of faith for the world. It appears to be immutable. It has always been here, 24 hours of every day, 365 days a year. Without the sun, people couldn't live. If the sun didn't rise tomorrow morning, what would happen to the world's faith? All of humanity would be thrown into confusion.

If we have such great faith in the sun, why don't we have even greater faith in the Son who made the sun and all the rest of the fixed order of the universe?

Our faith is in God. Genuine faith is born out of a knowledge of the will of God and exists only to fulfill that will. Faith is not a means of getting man's will done in heaven; it is the means of getting God's will done on earth.

After hearing me speak on spiritual conflicts, a young man came by to talk about his personal life. He said he'd had several experiences of not being able to speak the name of Jesus aloud. I asked him about his faith. He thought he had made a decision for Christ years earlier in an evangelistic meeting. He tried living with some American Indians to continue his spiritual journey, but that proved to be disastrous. He finally ended up living in a pastor's home where he was helped with the assurance of his salvation. This pastor believed in a "second work of grace," so he encouraged the young man to go into the woods and fight his lonely battle until he received it. Believing that he had, the young man reported this to the pastor. The pastor then encouraged him to just go live by faith.

The young man said to me, "I've been trying to live by faith for three years, and it has been one trial after another."

"Faith in what?" I asked.

He didn't know how to respond. This young man was trying to live by faith in faith. But faith itself is not a valid object. The only valid object for faith is God and the revelation we have of Him in His Word.

2. Faith Is Dependent Upon Knowing Its Object

How much faith we have is determined by how well we know the object of our faith. When my son, Karl, was a year old, I stood him on a table, backed away and told him to jump into my arms. He hesitated only momentarily, then with childlike faith he leaned forward and fell into my arms. As we repeated the activity, he became bolder and bolder. It wasn't long before he was jumping several feet into my arms.

At the age of two he was ready for the major leagues, so we moved from a table to the lower limb of a tree. It was a greater leap of faith to jump down into my arms from a tree, but he obediently did it. His faith in me continued to grow, provided I continued to catch him.

Suppose one day he jumped, but I didn't catch him. Would he climb up the tree and do it again? Probably not. Once faith is lost, it's hard to regain. One act of unfaithfulness in marriage will affect the relationship for years. The hurt spouse can forgive and decide to continue the relationship, but it will take a long time to re-establish the trust that was lost. Faith increases through repeated and ever larger steps of faith, provided the object of faith remains faithful.

Let's put my son back on the tree limb again. Instead of me catching him, I ask his older sister to catch him. Will he jump into her arms? Probably not, because I've changed the object of his faith. What happens if Karl climbs to the top of the tree? Will I continue to be a valid object for his faith? No! If he climbs high enough, there will be a point at which I will no longer be able to catch him.

There was a time when Karl thought I could answer any question or lick anybody (a confidence doomed to be shaken, since I'm neither omniscient nor omnipotent). There is only one who can catch him as he scales the higher limbs of life. It becomes my goal as a parent to remove myself as the ultimate object of his faith and introduce him to his heavenly Father. His identity must change from a child of Neil Anderson to a child of God. Then no matter how high God calls him, he will always be safe.

Big God, Big Faith

God doesn't change according to how we see Him. But there is a sense in which some today have a little God, while others have a big God. What makes the difference?

Paul writes, "So faith comes from hearing, and hearing by the word of Christ" (Romans 10:17). If we have little knowledge of God's Word we will have little faith. If we have a lot of knowledge of God's Word, we can have a lot of faith. The heroes in Hebrews 11 had great faith because they had a great God. Big God, big faith. Little God, little faith. If we know and put our trust in seven promises from Scripture, we have a seven-promise faith. If we know and believe seven thousand promises of Scripture, we have a seven-thousand-promise faith.

I'm not talking about being super intelligent as though only smart people can have faith. There are a lot of things in the Bible I don't understand, but I believe them. I don't fully understand the virgin birth, but I believe it.

You see, belief is a choice. We choose to believe what we have been convinced is true. Believing doesn't make it true, but it is true. Therefore, we believe.

Let me quickly add, however, that nobody (including myself) is presently living up to their faith potential. That's why we are to encourage one another in our faith. We are to encourage people to step out in faith according to what they already know to be true. Understanding increases with obedience. I may not know why God would have me do something, but as I commit myself to doing it, I often understand sometime later.

If God Wants It Done, It Can Be Done

Question! If God wants it done, can it be done? Yes! "All things are possible to him who believes" (Mark 9:23). If God wants me to do it, can I do it? Of course! "I can do all things through Him who strengthens me" (Philippians 4:13).

What are the "all things" mentioned in those verses? Is this "miracle-a-moment" living? Can we just name it and claim it? No. "All things" pertains to God's will. What God makes possible is the doing of His will; what He empowers us to do is what He desires done. Every miracle outside the will of God is made possible by the god of this world. Satan can work miracles, but he cannot please God. Notice the sobering warning of Jesus in Matthew 7:20-23:

> So then, you will know them by their fruits. Not every one who says to Me, "Lord, Lord," will enter the kingdom of heaven; but he who does the will of My Father who is in heaven. Many will say to Me on that day, "Lord, Lord, did we not prophesy in Your name, and in Your name cast out demons, and in Your name perform many miracles?" And then I will declare to them, "I never knew you; depart from me, you who practice lawlessness."

Jesus shocked His disciples when He cursed a fig tree which bore no fruit for Him. The next day Peter noticed the tree was withered from the roots up. When Peter pointed it out to Him, Jesus answered:

> Have faith in God. Truly I say to you, whoever says to this mountain, "Be taken up and cast into the sea," and does not doubt in his heart, but believes that what he says is going to happen, it shall be granted him. Therefore I say to you, all things for which you pray and ask, believe that you have received them, and they shall be granted you (Mark 11:22-24).

Can such a miraculous thing happen by prayer and faith? Yes, if we understand what a God-wrought miracle is. A miracle from God is a supernatural intervention in the fixed order of the universe for the sole purpose of establishing His kingdom. A true miracle can only be accomplished by God and only to help fulfill His redemptive purpose.

Moving a mountain into the sea fulfills no redemptive purpose. Besides, given enough time and earth-moving equipment, we could accomplish that without God. The point that Jesus is making is, "If God wants it done, it can be done." Nothing can keep us from doing the will of God, if we believe. Nobody can stop us from being the person God wants us to be. "Mountains" are often obstacles standing in the way of accomplishing God's will. Faith removes such barriers.

I'm sometimes impressed by how much the world can accomplish when they believe in themselves. When I worked on the Apollo space program in the 1960s, we bid on a contract for the space shuttle. The technology to build the type of rocket it would take to boost that size payload into space had not yet been developed, but NASA believed that given enough time and resources, it could be done. Ten years later it was. Some who believe only in science exhibit greater faith than Christians. How much more should we be able to accomplish if the object of our faith is God?

Even every commandment of God is a promise: "For as many as may be the promises of God, in Him they are yes" (2 Corinthians 1:20). God will never command us to do something that He will not also empower us to do. The will of God never leads us where the grace of God cannot enable us. It is never a question of whether God can, but if He wills. If He wills, then we can if we believe. Those predisposed to do His will understand what it is (John 7:17), and by the grace of God will do it.

It is critical to realize that God is under no obligation to man. God is only under obligation to Himself and to the covenants He has made with us. He will faithfully respond according to His Word which becomes operative in our lives when we choose to believe and act upon it. We don't need God jumping around in heaven catering to our every whim! There will never be a day when we say something and God has to do it because we said it. We cannot box God in.

There was a woman in my pastorate who wouldn't let me pray for her dying husband if I concluded my prayer with, "Be it done according to Thy will." I will never apologize for bowing to a higher authority. We are told to pray, "Thy will be done." Any other way would put us in the position of Lord. The misuse of God's Word and divine attributes is precisely how Satan tempted Jesus. Jesus withstood the temptation to act independently of God the Father and declared that His food was to do the will of His father who sent Him. That is our food as well.

3. Faith Results in Action

Faith is an action word. We cannot passively respond to God.

You may have heard the story of the circus performer who strung a wire over a river and proceeded to ride across it on a unicycle. When he returned, everyone applauded. Then he asked, "Who believes I can do that with a man on my shoulders?" Everyone responded in affirmation. He said, "All right, who will hop on?" The person who hops on is the person who really believes. Faith is not just giving credence to something or someone. Faith is a demonstrated reliance upon something or someone.

Faith has the same operating dynamic as *agape* love. When we refer to love as a noun, we're talking about character: "Love is patient, love is kind" (1 Corinthians 13:4). When we say that God is love, we are describing His character. Paul says the goal of our instruction is love (1 Timothy 1:5); therefore, the goal of Christian education is character transformation.

When love is used as a verb, it is expressed by action: "For God so loved the world that He gave" (John 3:16). If we say we love someone and do nothing on their behalf, it's only sentimentality and not *agape* love. True love is expressed by meeting the needs of others:

> We know love by this, that He laid down His life for us; and we ought to lay down our lives for the brethren. But whoever has this world's goods, and beholds his brother in need and closes his heart against him, how does the love of God abide in him? Little children, let us not love with word or with tongue, but in deed and truth (1 John 3:16-18).

Faith has a similar dynamic. When using faith as a noun, we're talking about what we believe. But if we're talking about faith as a verb, then it is expressed in the way we live. James says it like this:

> Even so faith, if it has no works, is dead, being by itself. But someone may well say, "You have faith, and I have works; show me your faith without the works, and I will show you my faith by my works." You believe that God is one. You do well; the demons also believe, and shudder (James 2:17-19).

The devil believes in the existence of Jesus and knows that God's Word is true. But he doesn't seek to glorify Jesus or to obey Him. He seeks his own glory, being a rebel at heart: "For they exchanged the truth of God for a lie, and worshiped and served the creature rather than the Creator" (Romans 1:25).

Let's go back to when I placed my son on the table and encouraged him to jump into my arms. What if Karl had never left that table, but kept insisting, "My daddy can catch me!" Does he really believe it? The answer is obvious. We demonstrate what we believe by how we live our lives. If we believe it, we will do it. If we don't do it, then what we believe is just wishful thinking.

Faith That Talks

One primary means by which we express our belief is confession—verbally expressing what we believe. In fact, God requires us to take our stand in this world. Jesus says:

> For whoever is ashamed of Me and My words in this adulterous and sinful generation, the Son of Man will also be ashamed of him when He comes in the glory of His Father with the holy angels (Mark 8:38).

The power of words is evident throughout the Bible: The worlds "were prepared by the word of God" (Hebrews 11:3); "By the word of the Lord, the heavens were made" (Psalm 33:6); "For He spoke and it was done; He commanded, and it stood fast" (Psalm 33:9); Jesus "upholds all things by the word of His power" (Hebrews 1:3).

Paul writes:

> If you confess with your mouth Jesus as Lord, and believe in your heart that God raised Him from the dead, you shall be saved; for with the heart man believes, resulting in righteousness, and with the mouth he confesses, resulting in salvation (Romans 10:9,10).

In rebuking the Pharisees, Jesus said, "For by your words you shall be justified, and by your words you shall be condemned" (Matthew 12:37). Look again at Mark 11:23:

> Truly I say to you, whoever says to this mountain, "Be taken up and cast into the sea," and does not doubt in his heart,

but believes that what he says is going to happen, it shall be granted him.

Notice that Jesus does not say we shall have whatever we believe, but we shall have whatever we believe and say. Confession gives expression to what is believed. It is the confession of the mouth that releases the belief of the heart.

When the disciples couldn't deliver a demon-possessed boy, Jesus said, "If you have faith as a mustard seed, you shall say to this mountain, 'Move from here to there,' and it shall move; and nothing shall be impossible to you" (Matthew 17:20). In Luke 17:6, Jesus said, "If you had faith like a mustard seed, you would say to this mulberry tree, 'Be uprooted and be planted in the sea,' and it would obey you." Jesus is revealing the power of faith when expressed in words.

I believe the primary purpose for speaking what we believe is to overcome the god of this world. Satan is under no obligation to obey our thoughts. He doesn't perfectly know them. Only God perfectly knows the thoughts and intentions of our heart (Hebrews 4:12). Satan can only observe our conduct, and having observed humanity for thousands of years, it's no great trick for him to figure out in a general way what we are thinking. We usually live out our thought life since every behavior is first preceded by a thought.

To defeat Satan, we must speak forth the Word of God, which is the sword of the Spirit (Ephesians 6:17). In our English translations, two different words are used for the "Word of God." The most common is *logos* and it indicates the whole revealed Word of God. For instance, Jesus is the *logos* in John 1:1. The other word is *rhema*. *Rhema* is the communication of *logos*. It is the same Word of God, but the emphasis of *rhema* is in its expression. We are to hide the whole Word (*logos*) in our hearts, and when Satan attacks, we stand against him by confessing God's Word (*rhema*).

Confessing what we believe gives proof of our faith. Confession doesn't create faith; faith makes possible true confession. Confession is agreeing with God. When we confess our sins, we are responding to the convictions of God and agreeing with Him about our moral condition. Forgiveness and cleansing come when we are in agreement with Him.

Satan will distort the truth of God and make confession a self-induced profession. The New Age movement teaches that something can become true if we believe it. In a similar fashion, the positive confession movement asserts that whatever we profess will become true. The emphasis has shifted from "Thy word is truth" to "My word is truth." "I said it, it must be true!" "I confessed it, so it must happen!" When this theology is questioned, the positive confessioners say that *logos* is the written Word of God, and *rhema* is the present revelation of God to their mind. When these modern-day "prophets" speak, they expect people to obey. When their authority is questioned, they respond, "Touch not God's anointed." When their inaccuracies are revealed, they say, "I'm only learning." If they had tried to pull that off in the Old Testament, they would have been stoned to death.

Satan will do all within his power to discredit God and undermine our confidence in His Word. But if there is a counterfeit, there must be a truth. If there are deceiving spirits, there must be a Holy Spirit who will lead us into all truth. Notice how we are to respond to the counterfeit and choose the truth:

> Beloved, do not believe every spirit, but test the spirits to see whether they are from God; because many false prophets have gone out into the world. You are from God, little children, and have overcome them; because greater is He who is in you than he who is in the world. . . . For whatever is born of God overcomes the world; and this is the victory that has overcome the world—our faith. And who is the one who overcomes the world, but he who believes that Jesus is the Son of God? (1 John 4:1,4; 5:4,5)

Faith Worth the Risk

The story is told of a prospector in the last century who had to make a four-day journey across a burning desert. He couldn't carry enough water to make the journey without dying of thirst, but he was assured there was a well halfway across the desert. So he set out, and sure enough there was a well right where the map indicated. But when he pumped the handle, the well only burped up sand. Then he saw this sign: "Buried two feet over and two feet down is a jug of water. Dig it up and use the water to prime the pump. Drink all the water you want, but when you are done, fill the jug again for the next person."

Sure enough, two feet over and two feet down was enough water for the prospector to prime the pump or to finish his two-day journey. Should he pour the water down the well or should he drink it?

To tell you the truth, I'd drink the water that was buried! I don't know who wrote the sign on that rusty old pump. It could be a cruel joke. I'd pour that water down a worthless well, only to watch my life drain away for lack of water.

I don't have to worry about things like that when it comes to trusting God. I know who wrote the sign. When I pour myself into a life of faith, I know that out of my inner being shall flow rivers of living water. God said so, history verifies it and I, for one, can testify that it is true. In the final analysis, God is not only true, He's right.

Is faith a risk? Of course. But failing to step out in faith is to risk missing life.

Risk

To laugh is to risk appearing the fool.
To weep is to risk appearing sentimental.
To reach out for another is to risk involvement.
To expose feelings is to risk exposing who we really are.
To place our ideas, our dreams before the crowd, is to risk
    their loss.
To love is to risk not being loved in return.
To live is to risk dying.
To hope is to risk despair.
To try is to risk failure.
Risks must be taken because the greatest hazard in life is to risk nothing. The person who risks nothing does nothing, has nothing, is nothing. He may avoid suffering and sorrow, but he simply cannot learn, feel, change, grow, love . . . live. Chained by his certitudes, he is a slave; he has forfeited freedom.

—Author Unknown

What a privilege for us to be able to walk by faith when the object of our faith is God Himself and all of the promises of His

Word. Let's express our gratitude and ask for His continuing guidance in prayer:

Dear Heavenly Father, You are the object of my faith. It is You I believe. You are the way, the truth and the life. By the counsel of Your will, all things hold together.

Forgive me for the times I acted presumptuously, thinking I was acting in faith. Forgive me for times when I didn't take Your Word seriously and failed to act when I know I should have.

I want to know You and know Your ways so I can walk by faith. I ask You to fill me with Your Spirit and guide me in the way of truth. I ask that You not lead me into temptation but deliver me from evil. I pray that You would never allow me to lead another person astray by my words or my example. As You direct my steps, may I glorify You in all that I do and say. Amen.

SPIRITUAL DISCERNMENT

I had dear friends who were being used by the Lord in full-time ministry. Some difficulty developed in their marriage so they consulted a pastor/counselor. The wife's response after the initial meeting was negative, but they continued with this particular counselor because other people they respected said he was a good man.

Over the next year the ministry my friends were in as well as our relationship deteriorated. A short time later their pastor/counselor was exposed for having sex with a number of counselees. The damage he did to several women was incredible. He justified his behavior by explaining, "What we do in the flesh doesn't matter. Only what we do in the spirit counts!"

My friends were confronted with an ultimatum by their ministry group: "Choose your ministry or choose him." They chose to stay with him!

Why won't people judge righteously? "Little children, let no one deceive you; the one who practices righteousness is righteous, just as He is righteous; the one who practices sin is of the devil" (1 John 3:7,8). The authoritative, arrogant spirit of this man had some kind of demonic hold on many, since half his church stayed with him. The initial discernment of my friends was correct, but they ignored the warning of the Holy Spirit.

157

I believe discernment is a critical part of our walk with God. This divine enablement is our first line of defense when our ability to reason is insufficient. Jesus demonstrated spiritual discernment throughout His earthly ministry. We need to examine His example and learn how to develop our ability to discern good from evil, truth from lies.

The Discernment of Jesus

While many Jews were questioning whether Jesus was a good man, they couldn't help but marvel at His teaching: "How has this man become learned, having never been educated?" (John 7:15) Jesus responded, "My teaching is not Mine, but His who sent Me" (John 7:16). (Would that we who teach the Bible could say that!)

After the Sermon on the Mount, the multitudes were amazed at His teaching, "for He was teaching them as one having authority, and not as their scribes" (Matthew 7:29). Jesus never had a formal education nor any secular position of authority, and still the skeptics recognized a teaching and authority not of this world.

Jesus also had the ability to discern beyond the normal means of external observation: "But Jesus, on His part, was not entrusting Himself to them, for He knew all men, and because He did not need anyone to bear witness concerning man for He Himself knew what was in man" (John 2:24,25).

It's not hard to know the truth if you are the truth, and speaking with authority would come quite natural if you're God! Discernment is also easier if you know, as Jesus does, what's in the hearts of men. Though we don't possess those attributes, we do have the Holy Spirit. If we are going to continue the work of Jesus, we must yield to the Holy Spirit and allow Him to possess us. Then we can know the truth, speak with authority and discern good and evil. Let's briefly analyze these three functions.

Our Guidance From the Spirit

First, *we have within us the Spirit of truth.* When Jesus promised to send the Holy Spirit, He said:

When He, the Spirit of truth, comes, He will guide you into all truth; for He will not speak on His own initiative, but whatever He hears, He will speak; and He will disclose to you what is to come. He shall glorify Me; for He shall take of Mine, and shall disclose it to you. All things that the Father has are Mine; therefore I said, that He takes of Mine, and will disclose it to you (John 16:13-15).

This promise has primary reference to the apostles, but its application extends to all Spirit-filled believers (1 John 2:20-27). The Holy Spirit is first and foremost a Spirit of truth, and He will lead us into all truth.

When Jesus prayed, He requested, "I do not ask Thee to take them out of the world, but to keep them from the evil one . . . Sanctify them in the truth; Thy word is truth" (John 17:15,17). Truth is what keeps us from the evil one. Truth is God's will made known through His Word. The Holy Spirit's role is to enable us to understand the Word of God from God's perspective. Because of His presence in our life, we incarnate the Word of God as we abide in Christ.

Second, *we can speak with authority.* The ability to do so stems from the same source as was true of Jesus Himself. The authority Jesus possessed was not based in any earthly position, but in the quality, conduct and character of His life.

The true shepherd exercises spiritual leadership with the heart of a servant. Spiritual leadership cannot be based in a position of authority since there is no position lower than a servant. We can speak with authority only when our character is Christ-like. As servants, we are subject to the needs of those we are called to lead. That's why He said we will know His disciples by their love. The requirements to be a spiritual leader in 1 Timothy 3 and Titus 1 are all character requirements. All of this is made possible by the indwelling presence of God the Holy Spirit. Peter writes:

Shepherd the flock of God among you, not under com- pulsion, but voluntarily, according to the will of God; and not for sordid gain, but with eagerness; nor yet as lording it over those allotted to your charge, but proving to be examples to the flock (1 Peter 5:2,3).

You never hear Jesus say, "You do this because I'm God." What happens to a marriage relationship when a husband authoritatively demands obedience because he is the head of the home? Nothing good, let me assure you. The spiritual head of a home assumes his responsibility by meeting the needs of his family. Being the head of a home is an awesome responsibility, not a right to be demanded. A wise husband listens carefully to the counsel of his wife and depends upon the Holy Spirit. With the Holy Spirit's enablement, he can live a righteous life out of which he can lead with loving authority.

Third, *the Holy Spirit enables us to discern.* According to John 16:8, He "will convict the world concerning sin, and righteousness, and judgment." The Holy Spirit doesn't take up residence in our lives and then sit passively by while we participate in sin. Since we are in Christ, we have become partakers of the divine nature (2 Peter 1:4), and we sense conviction when we choose to behave in a way that isn't consistent with the Spirit's presence in our lives. The Holy Spirit is not compatible with the world, the flesh or an evil spirit. The Holy Spirit enables us to discern good from evil.

How Discernment Comes

I don't know any legitimate Christian who questions the role of the Holy Spirit in leading us to truth or living a righteous life or helping us discern good from evil. The debate is not if He does, but how He does it. I would like to make some observations from 1 Corinthians 2:9-16:

> But just as it is written, "Things which eye has not seen and ear has not heard, and which have not entered the heart of man, all that God has prepared for those who love Him." For to us God revealed them through the Spirit; for the Spirit searches all things, even the depths of God. For who among men knows the thoughts of a man except the spirit of the man, which is in him? Even so the thoughts of God no one knows except the Spirit of God. Now we have received, not the spirit of the world, but the Spirit who is from God, that we might know the things freely given to us by God, which things we also speak, not in words taught by human wisdom, but in those taught by the Spirit, combining spiritual thoughts with

spiritual words. But a natural man does not accept the things of the Spirit of God; for they are foolishness to him, and he cannot understand them, because they are spiritually appraised. But he who is spiritual appraises all things, yet he himself is appraised by no man. For who has known the mind of the Lord, that he should instruct Him: But we have the mind of Christ.

Though this is a difficult passage to understand, I believe it's safe to draw the following conclusions. One, a natural man cannot discern what is spiritually true; he can only know his own thoughts. Two, the Holy Spirit knows all things and is capable of revealing the nature of God and His will. The Spirit of God knows the thoughts of God. Three, we have not received the spirit of the world but the Spirit who is from God. The Spirit makes known to us the things freely given by God. Four, we have the mind of Christ.

Five, the Holy Spirit takes words (*logos*), which are not taught by human wisdom but by the Spirit, and combines (brings together, compares or explains) them. What is actually being combined or compared is fuzzy, though, because the original language literally says, "spirituals with spirituals." The NASB translates that as "combining spiritual thoughts with spiritual words." The NIV translates it as "words taught by the Spirit, expressing spiritual truths in spiritual words."

The natural man looks like this:

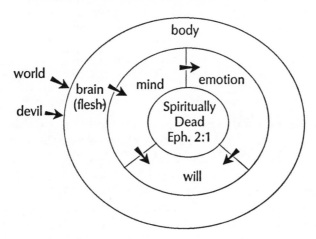

The natural man is spiritually dead, separated from God. He has neither the presence of God in His life nor the knowledge of God's ways. He has learned to live his life independently of God. Essentially, this is what constitutes the "flesh." His mind has been conformed to this world. The brain, which is physical and part of the body, functions like a computer. The mind is the programmer. The body picks up data from the world through its five senses. The mind chooses and interprets the data, and the brain stores it. The emotions are essentially a product of how the mind chooses to think and interpret life's events.

When we are born again, the Holy Spirit takes up residence in our life. Because we are now spiritually alive and united with Christ, we have the mind of Christ. We have become a partaker of the divine nature. However, nobody pushed the clear button in the computer. The brain is still programmed to live independently of God. The Christian now looks like this:

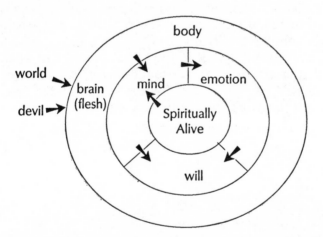

The battle is for the mind: "For the flesh sets its desire against the Spirit, and the Spirit against the flesh; for these are in opposition to one another" (Galatians 5:17). God has given us the responsibility to choose. The carnal Christian chooses to walk according to the flesh. What governs his behavior are the old habit patterns and thoughts that were programmed over time. The spiritually defeated Christian fails to put on the armor of God, and ends up paying attention to deceiving spirits. The spiritual man has crucified the flesh and put on the armor of God; he chooses to think upon that which is true.

We are to be renewed in the spirit of our minds (Ephesians 4:23). The Holy Spirit discloses the mind of Christ. We must choose to no longer be conformed to this world. We are to be diligent to present ourselves approved to God as a workman who does not need to be ashamed, handling accurately the word of truth (2 Timothy 2:15). When we do, we are transformed by the renewing of our minds. We choose to think the truth, and the Holy Spirit enables our thoughts and renews our minds with the *logos*. Then the peace of God guards our hearts and minds. We let the peace of Christ rule in our hearts by letting the word of Christ richly dwell in us (Colossians 3:15,16). We are now equipped to discern.

Distinguishing Right and Wrong

In a world saturated with deceiving spirits, false prophets and false teachers, the importance of exercising discernment cannot be overemphasized. In the Old Testament, the Hebrew word *bin* is used 247 times and is translated as "discern," "distinguish" and sometimes "understand." It means "to make a distinction, or separate from." The New Testament counterpart, *diakrino*, also means "to separate or divide." It is used primarily in reference to judging or making decisions. The Holy Spirit enables us to distinguish right from wrong, truth from lies, God's thoughts from man's thoughts.

An incident in Solomon's life is helpful in understanding discernment. David had died and Solomon had taken his place as king of Israel. Solomon admitted he felt too young and inexperienced to be the king: "And now, O Lord my God, Thou has made Thy servant king in place of my father David, yet I am but a little child; I do not know how to go out or come in" (1 Kings 3:7). In Gibeon the Lord appeared to Solomon in a dream at night, and God said, "Ask what you wish Me to give you." Solomon asked and the Lord responded:

> "Thy servant is in the midst of Thy people which Thou has chosen, a great people who cannot be numbered or counted for multitude. So give Thy servant an understanding heart to

judge Thy people to discern between good and evil. For who is able to judge this great people of Thine?" And it was pleasing in the sight of the Lord that Solomon had asked this thing. And God said to him, "Because you have asked this thing and have not asked for yourself long life, nor have asked riches for yourself, nor have you asked for the life of your enemies, but have asked for yourself discernment to understand justice, behold, I have done according to your words. Behold, I have given you a wise and discerning heart, so that there has been no one like you before you, nor shall one like you arise after you" (1 Kings 3:8-12).

This passage reveals several key concepts about discernment. First, *God gave Solomon the ability to discern because of the purity of his motives.* Solomon wasn't asking for personal gain or advantage over his enemies. He was asking for the ability to discern good and evil, and God gave it to him. The ability to discern is completely dependent upon God who is able to look at the heart. This is true for the proper use of any spiritual gift. Wrong motives open the door for Satan's counterfeits.

A few years ago, an undergraduate girl was following me around to various speaking engagements. After an evening service at a local church, she was shaking visibly. I saw her plight and asked if I could help. Learning she was a student, I asked her to stop by my office the next day. When we got together, she told me she was seeing one of our Christian counselors. I asked her how that was going, and she replied it was like a game. She could tell everything the counselor was going to do next. When I realized she enjoyed playing mind games with her counselor, I challenged her, "You like doing that, don't you? You like the advantage it gives you over other people." As soon as I exposed the deception, an evil spirit manifested itself.

She believed God had given her a spiritual gift that enabled her to point out people's sins. She could walk on campus and say, "That person is struggling with sex, that person with alcohol," etc. As near as I could tell, she was right. Yet when she found her freedom in Christ, the ability disappeared. That wasn't the Holy Spirit enabling her to discern. It was an evil spirit compatible with the evil spirits that were causing the moral problems in the other people. Her goal had been to go into counseling and use this "gift" to "help" people. Instead, she went to the mission field. Now she is helping people, but this time by the Spirit of God.

Second, this passage clearly establishes that *true biblical discernment is always on the plane of good and evil*. The distinguishing of spirits the Bible teaches is the Holy Spirit enabling us to distinguish between a good spirit and an evil spirit (1 Corinthians 12:10). I was working with a young lady who was plagued with compulsive thoughts that contributed to an eating disorder. As she was going through the process of forgiving others, I sensed that it wasn't the girl talking anymore. "That's not her," I said. There were several other people in the room observing the counseling process, but nobody else sensed it. They wondered how I knew. I don't know how I knew, but I knew. The fact that I was right was evident immediately. The expression on her face changed, and a voice said, "She will never forgive that person."

While spiritual discernment is primarily a function of the Spirit and not the mind, it doesn't bypass the mind, nor does it replace the need to know the truth from the Word of God. Rather, it builds upon the truth already understood in our hearts. There are numerous occasions when our minds want to know what's wrong. We may not receive the answer right away, but the Holy Spirit is alerting us that something is wrong—like a built-in alarm system.

Let me illustrate. Suppose my son comes home and I sense something is wrong. So I ask him, "What's wrong, Karl?" He says, "Nothing!" Again I ask him what's wrong, and again he claims nothing is wrong. My "buzzer" is going off because I am discerning that something is wrong. At this point we typically blow the discernment. We try to be objective, so we guess what it is. (Isn't that being objective?) "Karl, have you been doing such and such again?" If I guess wrong (and I probably will), I blow the discernment. Karl will stalk away into his room, mad at me for falsely charging him.

So what should I have done? Just share the discernment. "Karl, something is wrong." "No, Dad, nothing's wrong!" "Karl, I know something is wrong." He shrugs his shoulders and goes to his room. Is that it? No, that's not it! Remember, the Holy Spirit is going to convict the world of sin. The Holy Spirit made me aware that something is wrong and after I express that, God has a direct shot at Karl in his bedroom. Guess what happens in his room? Conviction! I can almost imagine what he is thinking— *Dad knows!* I really don't know what's wrong, but my discernment knows something is wrong.

When I was pastoring, I would sometimes enter a family's home and sense something was wrong. There was nothing visible. The people were smiling, they had a pot of coffee on and they had even dusted off the Bible. But I could cut the air with a knife. I knew something wasn't right, but I never knew what to do about it. We tend to ignore that kind of discernment and conduct business as usual. If we discern something is wrong, we should stop and pray. God can give us wisdom in knowing what to do. If we ignore the discernment, we will just continue ignoring the warning of the Holy Spirit.

Discernment, a Spiritual Weapon

Discernment is like an early warning system, the first line of defense in a spiritual world. There's nothing mystical about this. It makes sense that the Holy Spirit is not going to bear witness when an evil spirit is present: "You cannot drink the cup of the Lord and the cup of demons; you cannot partake of the table of the Lord and the table of demons" (1 Corinthians 10:21).

I can't imagine the Holy Spirit remaining passive in the face of adversity. But don't confuse this with human intuition. This is the Holy Spirit bearing witness with my spirit and counteracting the influence of the world, the flesh and the devil. When they are incompatible, the buzzer goes off. Perhaps you've had the positive experience of sensing a compatible spirit in a stranger whom you just "knew" was a Christian, even though nothing had been said.

Hebrews 5:12—6:2 offers further insight:

> For though by this time you ought to be teachers, you have need again for someone to teach you the elementary principles of the oracles of God, and you have come to need milk and not solid food. For every one who partakes only of milk is not accustomed to the word of righteousness, for he is

a babe. But solid food is for the mature, who because of practice have their senses trained to discern good and evil. Therefore leaving the elementary teaching about Christ, let us press on to maturity, not laying again a foundation of repentance from dead works and of faith toward God, of instruction about washings, and laying on of hands, and the resurrection of the dead, and eternal judgment.

What the writer of Hebrews identifies as elementary teaching is heavy theology for most people. A good systematic theology is the foundation upon which we build our lives. It is to our walk with God what our skeleton is to our body. It holds us together and keeps us in the right form. But right doctrine is never an end in itself. True doctrine governs our relationship with God and man. Many Christians have a relationship with God that is only theological, not personal. Those accustomed to the word of righteousness are sensitive to the personal leading of the Holy Spirit.

Solomon started with a love for God. He "became greater than all the kings of the earth in riches and in wisdom. And all the earth was seeking the presence of Solomon, to hear his wisdom which God had put in his heart" (1 Kings 10:23,24). He had the ability to discern, but moral demise led to his downfall. His wives turned his heart away, and he was no longer accustomed to the words of righteousness. His heart was not wholly devoted to the Lord, and the kingdom of God was torn in two.

Many Christians come faithfully to church on Sunday and the words sink into their ears, but not into their hearts. Their eyes aren't opened because their senses haven't been trained to discern good and evil.

I'm not sure my senses would have been trained if God hadn't called me into the ministry of setting captives free. If we are going to minister in a world of deception, we had better learn to rely upon God and not lean on our own understanding.

Discerning Specific Issues

The Holy Spirit is resident in our lives for more than warning. Sometimes He gives us impressions of what the problem really is. While ministering, it isn't uncommon to have thoughts come to my mind. For instance, a person could be sharing their story, and I'm sensing they are struggling with homosexuality. I never treat such impressions as authoritative; I test every one as I believe Scripture requires us to do. I do this by waiting for the right opportunity and ask something like this, "Have you ever struggled with homosexual feelings or tendencies?" If it triggers no response, I know the impression isn't valid or the person doesn't want to disclose it at this time. In either case, I continue to develop trust and understanding.

As I have matured in the Lord, I find that these impressions are generally true, and they get to the heart of the issue. But I never ascribe scriptural quality to them, nor do I believe they are a substitute for knowing the Bible. Our ability to discern grows in proportion to our spiritual maturity and knowledge of God and His ways. God brings to our minds the Scripture we have already put into our hearts through studying His Word. There are no shortcuts to maturity. The Holy Spirit doesn't bypass the parts of Scripture that require us to show compassion, develop trusting relationships and exercise patience. The spiritual leading of the Holy Spirit works through the whole counsel of God.

Deceiving spirits encourage shortcuts, bypass the mind and seek to create a dependency upon esoteric knowledge (knowledge that can only be understood by a few elite people). Spirit guides can give you the knowledge you seek by bypassing your mind. You won't even have to think. Just go by what you hear in your head. Sounds good, doesn't it? That's how a medium works. New Age channelers are making big money with their esoteric knowledge. Some will even profess to be Christians. Satan gives them enough truth to hook a gullible public.

John writes, "Beloved, do not believe every spirit, but test the spirits to see whether they are from God; because many false prophets have gone out into the world" (1 John 4:1). This is not optional. We are required by God to test the spirits. There is only one infallible source of faith and practice, and that's the Word of God. It's the *logos* hidden in our hearts that the Holy Spirit bears witness to.

Our power to perceive the light of God is, of all our powers, the one which we need most to cultivate and develop.

As exercise strengthens the body and education enlarges the mind, so the spiritual faculty within us grows as we use it in seeing and doing God's will.

—*Friends Book of Discipline*

Let's not waste such a precious resource that God has made available to us—our minds quickened by the Holy Spirit to be able to discern good and evil, right and wrong. If you desire to see your discernment strengthened, I invite you to pray with me:

Dear Heavenly Father, I desire to know You and Your ways. I don't want to take any shortcuts and be deceived by evil spirits. I want to know the truth and You are the truth. Teach me to think so as to have sound judgment. I want to base my leadership in character, not position, so I commit myself to be like You.

I want people to know me for my love. May that be the proof that I am Your disciple. Deliver me from a knowledge that would make me arrogant. I confess to You my pride. I humble myself before You and ask that You would fill me with Your Holy Spirit.

I ask You to lead me into all truth, so that I can discern good and evil. I ask for the courage to take my stand in the world, with the authority that comes from truth and righteousness. I ask this in the name of Jesus. Amen.

Part Three:

Walking
With God

If we find ourselves huffing and
puffing our way through life,
maybe we're not walking with God.

13

WALKING BY
THE SPIRIT

A young pilot had just passed the point of no return when the weather changed for the worse. Visibility dropped to a matter of feet as fog descended to the earth. Putting total trust in the cockpit instruments was a new experience to him, for the ink was still wet on the certificate verifying that he was qualified for instrument flying.

The landing worried him the most. His destination was a crowded metropolitan airport that he wasn't familiar with. In a few minutes he would be in radio contact with the tower. Until then, he was alone with his thoughts. Flying with no visibility, he became aware of how easy it would be to panic. Twice he reached for the radio to broadcast, "Mayday!" but he forced himself to go over and over the words of his instructor instead. His instructor had practically forced him to memorize the rule book. He didn't care for it at the time, but now he was thankful.

Finally he heard the voice of the air traffic controller. Trying not to sound apprehensive, the young pilot asked for landing instructions. "I'm going to put you on a holding pattern," the controller responded. *Great!* thought the pilot. However, he knew that his safe landing was in the hands of this person. He had to draw upon his previous instruction and training, and trust the voice of an air traffic controller he couldn't see. The words of an old hymn, "Trust and obey for there's no other way," took on new meaning. Aware that this was no time for pride, he informed the controller, "This is not a seasoned pro up here. I would appreciate any help you could give me." "You got it!" he heard back.

For the next forty-five minutes, the controller gently guided the pilot through the blinding fog. As course and altitude corrections came periodically, the young pilot realized the controller was guiding him around obstacles and away from potential collisions. With the words of the rule book firmly placed in his mind, and with the gentle voice of the controller, he landed safely at last.

The Holy Spirit guides us through the maze of life much like that air traffic controller. The controller assumed that the young pilot understood the instructions of the flight manual. His guidance was based on that. Such is the case with the Holy Spirit: He can guide us only if we have the knowledge of God's Word and His will established in our minds.

The Urgent Need

Early in church history, the Jerusalem council convened to discuss two critical issues that were threatening the body of believers (see Acts 15). One issue was circumcision and the other was socializing with the use of food. They were debating the boundaries of legalism and license. That tension still exists today.

It is important to note how the early Christians finally came to an agreement. First, they searched the Scriptures: "And with this the words of the prophets agree, just as it is written" (Acts 15:15). After consulting the Scriptures, they drafted a letter that was sent with Paul, part of which says, "They had become of one mind. . . . For it seemed good to the Holy Spirit and to us" (Acts 15:25,28). Their search for guidance through their crisis was balanced: They consulted the Scriptures and came to the mind of Christ by the aid of the Holy Spirit.

We desperately need God's guidance through the moral demise of our country today. But I'm puzzled at the evangelical response. We see divorce, so we preach against divorce. We see drunkenness, so we preach against the excessive use of alcohol.

We see drugs, so we preach against drugs. How's it working? Preaching morality never has worked and it never will! If we are only moralists, we aren't proclaiming the gospel. And jumping to the other extreme of whitewashing sin is equally devastating. The only balanced hope we have is stated in Galatians 5:16-18:

> But I say, walk by the Spirit, and you will not carry out the desires of the flesh. For the flesh sets its desire against the Spirit, and the Spirit against the flesh. For these are in opposition to one another, so that you may not do the things that you please. But if you are led by the Spirit, you are not under the law.

The flight instruction manual is the authoritative means by which we fly. But who would deny that the plane is empowered by something other than the pilot or question the need for an air traffic controller? In the same way, we sense our need for someone to guide us. The real difficulty lies not in the need, but in the "how to" of walking by the Spirit. If I answered the question with three steps and a formula, I'd be putting you back under the law. To walk by the Spirit is not a legal issue—it's a personal issue. The air traffic controller is a living personality, not a recorded message from a computer. The Holy Spirit is not an "it"; the Holy Spirit is a He.

It is easier to explain what walking by the Spirit is not, rather than what it is, so let's start with what it isn't.

Not Undisciplined Freedom

First, from the above passage in Galatians, we can clearly see that *walking by the Spirit is not license*. *License* is defined as an excessive or undisciplined freedom constituting the abuse of a privilege. It gave way to the old King James term, *licentious*, meaning lacking moral discipline with no regard for accepted rules and regulations. Paul says walking by the Spirit ensures that we don't carry out the desires of the flesh, and His presence guards against doing whatever we please.

When I was born, I was completely dependent upon my mother and father for human survival. If they hadn't fed me, changed me and taken care of me, I would have died. My goal as any little child was to be independent. Like most children, my striving for independence began with the "terrible twos." So my parents set parameters. They knew that for my safety, they simply could not let me do what I pleased.

Since I came into this world physically alive but spiritually dead, I learned to live my life independent of God. Essentially, that is what constitutes the flesh. I had neither the presence of God in my life nor the knowledge of God's ways, so I learned to cope and defend myself as I was being conformed to this world. This learned independence is what makes the flesh hostile toward God. That is why the flesh and the Spirit are in opposition to one another.

Being children of God, the presence of the Holy Spirit restrains us so we will not do the things that we please. If there were no moral restraints and no boundaries to govern our behavior, we would drive ourselves into moral decadence. Imagine the air traffic controller saying to the pilot, "You have my permission to land any time and any place you want." That pilot would most likely crash and burn!

Paul writes, "You were called to freedom, brethren, only do not turn your freedom into an opportunity for the flesh, but through love serve one another" (Galatians 5:13). God wants us free, but freedom is not license. I believe we are free by the grace of God to live a responsible life. In the early part of the twentieth century, a rigid fundamentalism had left our churches frozen in legalism. In the '50s it began to thaw, and the Jesus People movement of the '60s and '70s melted it into license for many. The pendulum had swung from the justice of God to the mercy of God. "God loves me," believers reasoned, "so I can do whatever I want. There's no way He would send me to hell." A libertine spirit led to free sex and free drugs. The result is a society on the brink of disaster.

There's always a price to pay for license. True freedom doesn't lie in the exercise of choices, but in the consequences of the choices made. You may reserve the right to tell a lie, but you'll be in bondage to it because you'll have to remember the nature of the lie and to whom you told it. You may choose to rob a bank, but you will always be looking over your shoulder, fearing you may be caught. That's bondage.

If we choose to walk by the flesh, we are responsible for the consequences of the choices we make. If we walk by the Spirit, God says He assumes responsibility for the consequences.

Not Chained by the Law

Second, *walking by the Spirit is not legalism:* "But if you are led by the Spirit, you are not under the law" (Galatians 5:16).

If we choose to relate to God on the basis of the law, then we need to be aware of three biblical truths. First, the law will function as a curse. Look at Galatians 3:10-14:

> All who rely on observing the law are under a curse, for it is written: "Cursed is everyone who does not continue to do everything written in the Book of the Law." Clearly no one is justified before God by the law, because, "The righteous will live by faith." The law is not based on faith; on the contrary, "The man who does these things will live by them." Christ redeemed us from the curse of the law by becoming a curse for us, for it is written: "Cursed is everyone who is hung on a tree." He redeemed us in order that the blessing given to Abraham might come to the Gentiles through Christ Jesus, so that by faith we might receive the promise of the Spirit (NIV).

If we want to base our relationship with God on how well we keep the law, we should first consider James 2:10: "For whoever keeps the whole law and yet stumbles on one point, he has become guilty of all." Thankfully, our relationship with God is based on who we are in Christ, not on our ability to keep the law. We are not saved by how we perform, but by how we believe: "For the law has become our tutor to lead us to Christ that we may be justified by faith" (Galatians 3:24). The blessings of Abraham have come to the Gentiles because we are alive, right now, in Christ Jesus. Look again at Galatians 3:14: "He redeemed us in order that the blessing given to Abraham might come to the Gentiles through Christ Jesus, so that by faith we might receive the promise of the Spirit" (NIV). We are recipients of the Holy Spirit through faith and He is operative in our life through faith.

Many Christians labor under the moral fog of legalism. To them the gospel isn't good news, it's bad news. They don't go to church to celebrate what Christ has already done; they go to receive another dose of guilt. Legalistic pastors know no other way to keep their people within the moral boundaries of Scripture other than holding them over the fires of hell and threatening, "Turn or burn." These types of pastors are moralists. They focus on the external, not the internal. They quote, "As a man thinks in his heart, so is he," but all they see is the "so is he." Their entire focus is to change behavior.

What they fail to understand is that the real battle is for the mind. People's thoughts determine what they do. We need to find out what's happening on the inside, then we will know why people are behaving the way they are. The moralist looks only on the outside of man, but Jesus looks upon the heart.

The second limitation of the law is that it is powerless to give life. Telling people that what they are doing is wrong does not give them the power to stop. In and of itself, the law is impotent:

> Is the law then contrary to the promises of God? May it never be! For if a law had been given which was able to impart life, then righteousness would indeed have been based on law (Galatians 3:21).

We were dead in our trespasses and sins, but now we are alive in Christ: "We are servants of a new covenant, not of the letter, but of the Spirit. For the letter kills, but the Spirit gives life" (2 Corinthians 3:6). This life establishes our true identity as to whom we are as children of God. Jesus said, "I came that you might have life and have it more abundantly" (John 10:10).

Not Slaves to Sin

No person can consistently behave in a way that is inconsistent with how he perceives himself: "And every one who has this hope fixed on Him purifies himself, just as He is pure" (1 John 3:3). The gospel says that we are not just forgiven but that we have become new creations in Christ. God changed our nature, but it is our responsibility to change our behavior. I'm not whitewashing sin; I'm trying to establish how God intends us to be free from it: "Knowing this, that our old self was [past tense] crucified with Him, in order that our body of sin might be done away with that we should no longer be slaves to sin" (Romans 6:6).

In order to live a life free from sin, we have to understand an important fact. A grim determination of our will to overcome sin won't work if we keep insisting that Christians are still sinners. Because what do sinners do? They sin! The Bible doesn't call the child of God a sinner; it calls the child of God a saint who sins.

The third startling fact about the law is that it can stimulate the desire to do that which it tries to prohibit. Try telling a child he can go one place but not another, and where does he want to go immediately? When I was young, I had some friends who were Catholic. Their church posted a list of movies they couldn't see which quickly became a list of movies to see. My friends actually tore the list off the wall of the church and shared it with the entire high school campus.

According to Romans 7:5, some sinful passions are actually aroused by the law: "For while we were in the flesh, the sinful passions, which were aroused by the law, were at work in the members of our body to bear fruit for death." Paul argues in Romans 7 that the law isn't sinful, even though it stimulates the desire to sin:

> What shall we say then? Is the law sin? May it never be! But sin, taking opportunity through the commandment, produced in me coveting of every kind; for apart from the law sin is dead (Romans 7:7,8).

I'm not trying to tell you we shouldn't have a moral standard! Of course we need a moral standard. But the means by which we relate to God is by faith, and the presence of the Holy Spirit will enable us to walk between the two extremes of legalism and license.

The Christian life is like a journey down a road. The Holy Spirit provides sanctuary for those who walk the narrow path. To the right of the path is a sharp drop. It's a tempting option. You could sail off that cliff and enjoy an exhilarating "flight." But that kind of freedom has serious consequences—especially when you hit the bottom! Wanting to have my own way and demanding my "right" for freedom of choice without considering the consequences is license. It's a deadly step in the wrong direction.

To the left of that road is a roaring fire of legalism. The "accuser of the brethren" has a field day with those who choose to deviate from the narrow path by going back under the law. Many are burned by legalism. If you are led by the Spirit, you are not under the law: "There is no condemnation for those who are in Christ Jesus" (Romans 8:1).

So if walking by the Spirit is not license, and it's not legalism, then what is it? It is liberty: "Now the Lord is a Spirit, and where the Spirit of the Lord is there is liberty" (2 Corinthians 3:17). So how do we experience this liberty? It's in the walking.

Moving With God

Walking by the Spirit implies two things that it's not. First, walking by the Spirit is not sitting passively expecting God to do everything. And second, it is not running around in endless, exhausting activities as though everything depended on our efforts. Do you know how much would get accomplished for the kingdom of God if we expected God to do everything? Nothing! Do you know how much gets accomplished for the kingdom of God if we try to do it all by ourselves? Nothing! You and I have the privilege to water and plant, but God causes the increase. Yet if there is no watering or planting, there is no increase.

There was a pastor whose favorite hobby was gardening. One day a neighbor walked by and said, "The Lord sure gave you a beautiful garden." The pastor responded, "This garden is the Lord's and mine. You should have seen this plot of ground when the Lord had it all by Himself."

In counteracting Pharisaic slavery, Jesus said, "Come to Me all who are weary and heavy-laden, and I will give you rest. Take My yoke upon you and learn from Me, for I am gentle and humble in heart, and you shall find rest for your souls. For my yoke is easy and my load is light" (Matthew 11:28-30).

Jesus is alluding to the yoke that harnessed two oxen together. When a young ox was being broken in, it was paired with a lead ox. After much training, the lead ox knew the best way to accomplish a day's work was to neither run nor sit. He knew they would accomplish more if they walked down the narrow row, looking neither to the left nor to the right. And if the team was going to accomplish anything, they had to pull together.

Young oxen get impatient with the slow pace and want to run ahead. Do you know what they get? A sore neck! Other young oxen feel like doing nothing and just sit. Guess what they get? A sore neck. That lead ox is going to keep right on walking, no matter what the young ox does. Life has a way of continuing on whether we like it or not. Count on Jesus, our lead ox, to continue a steady pace down the center of that narrow path.

We had a perfect family dog that grew up with our children. When little Missy died, it was traumatic for us. I hurried to a pet store the same day and bought a replacement dog. Much like marrying on the rebound, it was a disaster. Buster grew up to be a DAWG! He is the most neurotic mess I've ever seen. My son signed up for twelve lessons of dog-obedience, but after two weeks it was my son who was thoroughly trained by Buster!

I tried putting a choke-chain around that dog and taking it for a walk. I had one conviction firmly planted in my mind: I was the master, and I was going to set the direction and pace of our walk. That dumb dog, however, wanted to run. He would strain at the end of the leash and choke all the way through our walk. Occasionally, Buster would stop and do his own thing. I kept on walking, however, and Buster would be choked into reality. Sometimes he would stray off the path and end up winding his leash around a tree. The result was like a wild ride at an amusement park as I kept on walking. Did the dumb dog ever learn to walk obediently by my side? No, he never did. I've known a few Christians like that.

Jesus said, *Come to Me. I'm the lead ox. Is your Christian life weary and heavy-laden? I'll give you rest. Take My yoke.* The flesh quickly responds, "That's all I need is another yoke!" But you can't put on the yoke of Christ without throwing off the yoke of legalism and license. *Learn from Me,* Jesus says. If we walked with Jesus, what do you think we would learn? To start with, we would learn to take one day at a time. We would learn the priority of relationships. We would learn that our walk is one of faith and not sight . . . one of grace, not legalism.

My yoke is easy, and My load is light, Jesus says. If we find ourselves huffing and puffing our way through life, maybe we're not walking with God. Maybe we're running in the flesh. I ask myself that very often. This is the only passage in the New Testament where Jesus describes himself. And He says He's gentle and humble in heart. We need to share the yoke with the gentle Jesus and pull together with Him: "As you therefore have received Christ Jesus, so walk in Him" (Colossians 2:6).

Following Our Guide

We not only walk by the Spirit, but we are led by the Spirit as well. Being led by the Spirit also implies two things that it's not. First, we are neither being pushed nor pulled. And second, we are neither driven (legalism), nor are we lured away (license).

There are a lot of driven Christians who know little of resting in the Spirit. Motivated by guilt, they can't say no. They expend a lot of energy, but they bear very little fruit. They measure success in ministry by the number of activities. They measure spirituality by the expenditure of human energy.

I've had people push me for an answer—now! I find it very easy to respond, "No." "Why not?" they ask. "Because God doesn't lead that way," I answer. The devil leads that way. He always demands an answer right now and withdraws the offer if time for consideration is requested. The guidance of God may come suddenly, but it never comes to the unprepared. Pentecost was sudden, but the disciples had spent days in prayerful preparation.

Many believers are lured away by various impulses. The lure of knowledge and power has trapped some. As undisciplined and lazy people, though, they don't want to study to show themselves approved. They accept the esoteric knowledge of the occult. They want the air traffic controller to explain the instruction manual to them while they are in the air. Why study when you can receive your knowledge from God directly? Others are pulled off the path by the lure of incredible power. They don't seem to understand the fact that they already have the power. It is the truth they need. Satanists pursue power; Christians pursue truth.

Growing up on a farm, I had the privilege of raising championship sheep. I can tell you from experience that sheep are not the smartest animals on the farm. They're right down there with chickens. For instance, you can self-feed cattle and pigs, but you can't sheep. If you turn sheep lose in a green pasture, they will literally eat themselves to death. One thing's for certain: Sheep without a shepherd will soon perish.

In the Western world, we drive our sheep from the rear, much like the Australians who use sheep dogs. However, that is not the case in Israel. In my trips to the Holy Land, I observed that the herds of sheep were generally small, and the shepherd would sit patiently by while the flock grazed. The shepherd seemed to have personal knowledge of every sheep. When an area was sufficiently grazed, the shepherd would say something and walk off. To my amazement, the sheep all looked up and followed him. What a beautiful illustration of what the Lord said in John 10:27: "My sheep hear My voice, and I know them, and they follow Me."

Walking by the Spirit is neither legalism nor license. It's not sitting passively, waiting for God to do something, nor is it running around in endless, exhausting circles trying to do everything by ourselves. If we walk by the Spirit, we are neither driven nor lured off the path of faith.

Walking by the Spirit is walking with God: "For all who are being led by the Spirit of God, these are the sons of God" (Romans 8:14). It's not a legal issue; it's a personal issue.

Would you pray with me for the peace and fulfillment of a life that simply keeps pace with God?

Dear Heavenly Father. You are the strength of my life. Forgive me for trying to fly alone. I not only need Your strength, but I also need Your guidance. I accept the times You put me in a holding pattern. I now realize that it was for my own good.

I desire to walk the narrow path, so I gladly accept Your

invitation to come to Jesus. I take His yoke upon me, and I throw off the yokes of legalism and license.

I commit myself to know Your Word so I can be guided by You. I no longer expect You to guide me without Your Word richly dwelling within me. And I no longer lean on my own understanding.

Lead me not into temptation, but deliver me from evil. Help me to know You so well that I can discern Your voice from the voice of the evil one.

I desire the liberty that comes only as I submit to You. I acknowledge my dependency upon You. I ask You to fill me with Your Holy Spirit that I may be led by You.

You are my God and I am a sheep in Your pasture. I love the security that comes from knowing You are my Shepherd. Amen.

WALKING IN THE LIGHT

Even as a young Christian, I realized that prayer was a vital link for God's guidance. But prayer was also the most frustrating part of my early Christian experience.

At seminary I remember reading about great saints who would spend two, three or four hours in prayer—sometimes even all night. I was struggling to spend five minutes! I would labor through my prayer list for two or three minutes then glance at my watch. I would wonder what was I going to say for the next two minutes. Prayer was supposed to be a dialogue with God, but for me it seemed like I was talking to the wall.

My greatest struggle was trying to stay focused. I knew what I wanted to pray about and I had my list, but distracting thoughts were a fierce competition. Every activity of the day was parading through my mind or pesky thoughts were reminding me of my many temptations. I would spend a lot of time rebuking Satan, assuming he was trying to distract me from my devotional life.

If prayer is so important, why is it so difficult?

In church we arranged our chairs in little circles. If the second person to pray happened to be seated by the first person who prayed, a pattern had been established: Each person would have to pray in turn as we went around the circle. But what if a person didn't pray when it was his turn and you were expected to follow that person? My thoughts were, *Why isn't that guy praying?* In the awkward silence I would wonder how long I should wait before I skipped him.

And did the next person to pray ever listen to the prayer of the previous person? Probably not. They were too concerned with what they were going to say when it was their turn. And then there was always the one who droned on and on and on, who everyone wished would stop praying! They never heard that long prayers are for the closet and short prayers are for public, and the devil will orchestrate the opposite.

When the opportunity came for me to pray the pastoral prayer in the morning service, it wasn't long before I realized, *I'm not talking to God. I'm talking to the people.* Initially, I was more conscious of the congregation's presence than I was of the presence of God. I found myself summarizing the sermon or giving the week's announcements in the prayer: "Dear Lord, bless our church picnic next Saturday at 9 A.M. at the city park on the corner of Fifth and Central, and help us to remember that last names beginning with A through G are to bring salads." That was no prayer; that was an announcement. One pastoral staff member would pray in King James English for so long that people were timing him: "Would you believe eleven minutes this morning!"

I don't want to make fun of prayer, but where is the reality? When we pray publicly, what are we modeling?

Realizing that prayer was important for my marriage, my wife and I would spend time discussing what we needed to pray about: "Let's pray about this, and we need to pray about this." After a lengthy discussion, we would pray by going through the same list again, only this time we would include God. I began to wonder where God was the first time we went through the list!

I know that God accepts and appreciates even our feeble efforts, but I sometimes wonder what He thinks. He's probably saying, "Why don't you just include Me from the beginning?" or "There they go around the prayer circle again. Come on, people, get real!"

Praying With Thanksgiving

I reached a turning point in my first ministry when I was doing a series of lessons on prayer. The first five lessons were theological, so I had little problem preparing for them, and I had determined well in advance that the last lesson would be, "How to Pray in the Spirit." But the night before I was to give that talk, I became acutely aware that I didn't have the foggiest idea how to pray in the Spirit. I was hours away from giving a message I personally couldn't relate to. I sat bankrupt before God. Those are special moments if you never have been there!

Sometime before midnight the Lord began to direct my thoughts through the Bible in one of the most important evenings of my life. I reasoned, *If I'm going to pray in the Spirit, I must be filled with the Spirit.* So I went to Ephesians 5:18-20:

> Do not get drunk with wine, for that is dissipation, but be filled with the Spirit, speaking to one another in psalms, and hymns and spiritual songs, singing and making melody in your heart to the Lord, always giving thanks for all things in the name of our Lord Jesus Christ, even the Father.

I leafed over to the parallel passage in Colossians 3:15-17:

> Let the peace of Christ rule in your hearts, to which indeed you were called in one body and be thankful, and let the Word of Christ richly dwell within you, with all wisdom, teaching and admonishing one another with psalms, and hymns, and spiritual songs, singing with thankfulness in your hearts to the Lord, and whatever you do in word or deed, do all in the name of our Lord Jesus Christ giving thanks to Him and to God the Father.

I noticed that being filled with the Spirit and letting the Word of Christ richly dwell within us was closely associated with the concept of giving thanks. I looked ahead to Colossians 4:2: "Devote yourselves to prayer keeping alert in it with an attitude of thanksgiving." Then Philippians 4:6: "Be anxious for nothing, but by prayer and supplication, with thanksgiving . . . ." I turned to 1 Thessalonians 5:17,18: "Pray at all times without ceasing and in everything giving thanks for this is God's will for you in Christ Jesus." Prayer and thanksgiving seemed to be bound together.

That evening I walked through the Epistles and this is what I found:

> I do not cease giving thanks for you while making mention of you in my prayers (Ephesians 1:16).
>
> I thank my God in all my remembrance of you always offering prayer (Philippians 1:3,4).
>
> We give thanks to God the father of our Lord Jesus Christ, praying always for you (Colossians 1:3).
>
> We give thanks to God always for all of you making mention of you in our prayers (1 Thessalonians 1:2).
>
> First of all then I urge that entreaties and prayers and petitions and thanksgivings be made on behalf of all men (1 Timothy 2:1).
>
> I thank God, whom I serve with a clear conscience, the way my forefathers did, as I constantly remember you in my prayers day and night (2 Timothy 1:3).
>
> I thank my God always making mention of you in my prayer (Philemon 1:4).

I turned to one of my favorite Old Testament passages, Psalm 95:

> Oh come let us sing for joy to the Lord, let us shout joyfully to the Rock of our salvation, let us come before His presence with thanksgiving. Let us shout joyfully to Him with psalms for the Lord is a great God, and a great king above all Gods, in whose hands are the depths of the earth, the peaks of the mountains are His also, the sea is His for it was He who made it and His hands formed the dry land. Come, let us worship and bow down, let us kneel before the Lord our maker, for He is our God and we are the people of His pasture and the sheep of His hand. Today if you would hear His voice . . .

The last three words grabbed me: "Hear His voice." I thought, *Today I'd love to hear Your voice!* Maybe I wasn't hearing His voice because I wasn't coming before Him with an attitude of thanksgiving.

In Psalm 95:7, the word *hear* is the Hebrew word *shema*, which means to "hear as to obey." Verse 8 quickly follows, "And do not harden your hearts." I turned to Hebrews 4:7 which quotes Psalm 95: "Today if you hear His voice, do not harden your hearts." I then read of the "Sabbath rest that remains" in Hebrews 4. It is an exhortation to cease trusting in our own works and begin to trust in God's. Resting in the finished work of Christ didn't typify my prayer time. I became painfully aware that my prayer time was a work of the flesh. It was not saturated with an attitude of thanksgiving and praise for all that He had, was and would do in my life.

Praying What God Wants Prayed

That same night I turned to Romans 8:26,27:

> In the same way the Spirit also helps our weakness, for we do not know how to pray as we should, but the Spirit Himself intercedes for us with groanings too deep for utterance. And He who searches the heart knows what the mind of the Spirit is, because He intercedes for the saints according to the will of God.

We really don't know how to pray or what to pray for, but the Holy Spirit does and He will help us in our weakness. *Help* is a fascinating word in Greek (*sunantilambano*), two prepositions placed in front of the word *take*. The Holy Spirit comes along side, bears us up and takes us to the other side. The Holy Spirit connects us with God. He intercedes for us on our behalf. The prayer that the Holy Spirit prompts us to pray is the prayer that God the Father will always answer.

How does the Holy Spirit help us in our weakness? I didn't know, but I tried something that evening. I said, "Okay Lord, I'm setting aside my list, and I'm going to assume that whatever comes to my mind during this time of prayer is from You or allowed by You. I'm going to let You set the agenda." Whatever came to my mind that evening was what I prayed about. If it was a tempting thought, I talked to God about that area of weakness. If the busyness of the day clamored for attention, I discussed my plans with God. I dealt with whatever came to my mind.

I wasn't passively letting thoughts control me, though. I was actively taking every thought captive to the obedience of Christ (2 Corinthians 10:5). Let me warn you that if you passively listen to your thoughts, you may end up paying attention to a deceiving spirit (1 Timothy 4:1).

If my mind entertained a lying thought or an evil thought, I didn't ignore it. I brought it before the Lord. It doesn't make any difference whether our thoughts come from an external source or from our preprogrammed past or from a deceiving spirit, we are still responsible to take every thought captive to the obedience of Christ. If an evil thought was coming from Satan, God was allowing it. In my experience, it typically identified an area of weakness that I had not previously been honest with God about. God will allow us to get banged around by Satan until we bring our struggles before the only one who can resolve them.

In my personal prayer, I was trying to shove evil thoughts away without much success. When I brought them to the light, it was amazing how much freedom I had. All the issues I was trying to ignore during prayer were issues God wanted me to deal with. He wanted to make me aware of matters that were affecting our personal relationship. Now when there is a tempting thought, I go naked before God and don't try to hide my human frailty.

Warning: If you try this, you will find out how personal God really is. Now you know why the phrase, "Today if you would hear His voice," is followed by, "Do not harden your heart." If God determined and prioritized our prayer list, He would begin with personal issues that affect our relationship with Him. "Come on," God says. "You keep telling others you have a personal relationship with Me. Let's get personal!"

I have challenged hundreds of seminary students to take a walk with God for forty-five minutes during class. They start their walk by thanking God for all He has done for them. I encourage them to take their Bible and a pad of paper to write down what comes to mind. I then instruct them to deal with those issues by bringing them before the Lord. If nothing comes to mind, they are to reflect upon God's goodness and thank Him for all He has done for them. I've had students return and tell me they accomplished more in that forty-five minutes than they ever had in their prayer life before. Some have dealt with personal issues never before discussed with God. Almost all have found it a refreshing encounter.

God Seeks Intimacy With Us

Fellowship with God is not an abstract theological concept, but a living relationship. Living in continuous agreement with God is to walk in the light: "If we walk in the light as He Himself is in the light, we have fellowship with one another, and the blood of Jesus His Son cleanses us from all our sin" (1 John 1:7). Satan can't accuse me if I live in the light, but walking in the light is not moral perfection: "If we say that we have no sin, we are deceiving ourselves" (1 John 1:8). The confession mentioned in 1 John 1:9 is agreeing with God about our present moral condition before Him.

What makes it possible to be this open with God about our condition is the fact that we are already His children. Our eternal state is not at stake, only our daily victory. We don't have to pretend with God in hopes that He will accept us. As children we're already accepted, so we are free to be honest with Him. We have no relationship to lose, only fellowship to gain. Knowing that we're secure in Christ, we can express ourselves honestly to Him. He already knows the thoughts and intentions of our hearts (Hebrews 4:12).

Have you ever wondered why it's so difficult to sit in the presence of God? God is our Father, and like any parent He doesn't appreciate grumbling, complaining children, especially since this Father sacrificed His only begotten Son for us. He will not be very interested in our list of demands if we haven't been obedient to Him. I also don't think He is going to be very interested in helping us develop our own kingdoms when we are to work at establishing the only one that will last—His!

To sit in the presence of my Father who loves me, who has made an incredible sacrifice so I can be there, doesn't have to be a dismal, failing experience. Listen to the heart of our heavenly Father:

> For we do not have a high priest who cannot sympathize with our weaknesses, but one who has been tempted in all things as we are, yet without sin. Let us therefore draw near with confidence to the throne of grace that we may receive mercy and may find grace to help in the time of need (Hebrews 4:15,16).

Let us draw near with a sincere heart in full assurance of faith, having our hearts sprinkled clean from an evil conscience (Hebrews 10:22).

Rest assured that a personal God is first concerned about the condition of our hearts. He encourages us to pray, "Our Father Who art in heaven."

The Natural Progression of Prayer

In my eighteen years of ministry, I have observed three approaches to prayer which progress from level to level. The first level is *petition*. We are encouraged to let our requests be made known to God (Philippians 4:6,7), though some never get beyond personal petitions. Often our petitions reflect the burdens that God has placed on our hearts. If it helps us to keep a list of daily prayer reminders, we should do so. However, most people weary of this, and their devotional life disappears over time. Often they don't see immediate results from their prayers, so they conclude that more can be accomplished if they just get busy for the Lord.

Of the ones who persist, many are motivated by guilt because they know that prayer is a Christian duty. I'm convinced that God is pleased with their efforts, although they are not as effective as they could be. He certainly is more pleased with them than with those who quit.

We've progressed to the second level when prayer becomes *personal*. We have discovered a new dimension when we are comfortable in His presence and don't feel obligated to talk. It's much like a marriage relationship. A mature couple can ride together in the car for hours, enjoying each other's company, without having to say a thing. But have you noticed how different it is when you're alone with a stranger? Silence is awkward.

It's okay to remain silent in God's presence. Realizing that I need not feel obligated to keep the conversation going when I'm with God changed my prayer life dramatically. I can walk with God as long as I walk in the light. I can commune with Him as I drive to work. This kind of prayer makes my relationship with God a 24-hour-a-day experience. Setting aside special times is still important, but when I leave my quiet times, God doesn't stay there and He doesn't go with me—rather I go with Him!

I call the third dimension of prayer *true intercession.* True intercessors hear from God. They know how to pray and what to pray for. In my observation there are very few true intercessory prayer warriors. The ones I know of are usually older than fifty, and most are ladies. They pray privately in their homes and often at night. God wakes them up, and they know who and what to pray for. These warriors often invite others for prayer in their home, and they'll pray through problems for as long as it takes. If you are a pastor, find out who the prayer warriors are in your congregation. Every church has at least one or two of them. Share your schedule and family needs with them. When these people pray, things happen.

Praise and thanksgiving are part of every level of prayer. They are continuous as we walk in the light. To come before God with thanksgiving is no different than coming before our earthly parents with an attitude of gratitude. Nothing disturbs a parent more than a child who is always demanding, forever complaining and never satisfied. How would you feel if you've given as much as you can as a parent and your child still wants more, more, more? On the other hand, how would you feel toward the child who snuggles up and says, "Thanks for being who you are. I just love you and I know you're doing the best you can for me." What a great parent-child relationship.

Praising God is simply describing His attributes. I try to be aware when I pray that God is the ever-present, all-powerful, all-knowing, loving heavenly Father. I don't praise Him because He needs me to tell Him who He is. He knows who He is. I am the one who needs to keep His divine attributes constantly in my mind. And the knowledge of God's presence is foremost in my thoughts. No matter where I go, He is with me.

I'm always disturbed when I hear people asking God to "be there." What a blatant denial of His omnipresence. The same goes for asking God to be with our missionaries. We have the assurance of Scripture that He will be with them unto the ends of the earth. We can confidently acknowledge that He will neither leave us nor forsake us. We ought to thank God for His presence and ask Him to bring to our minds anything that may be keeping us from having perfect fellowship with Him.

Choosing Truth, Dispelling Darkness

When prayer becomes personal, the Christian's life corresponds with the level of growth depicted in 1 John 2:14:

> I write to you, young men, because you are strong, and the word of God lives in you, and you have overcome the evil one (NIV).

Until you have overcome the evil one, you may not have a lot of mental peace. If you are attempting to deal with deceiving thoughts by trying to rebuke them, you'll be like the person treading water in the middle of the ocean whose whole life purpose is to keep twelve corks which are bobbing close by submerged with a little hammer! Acknowledge the presence of the corks, but ignore them and swim to shore! Don't pay attention to deceiving spirits.

The whole thrust of Scripture is to choose truth. We dispel the darkness by turning on the light. If you are plagued by tempting thoughts, bring the issue before God and seek to resolve that which is keeping you from having perfect fellowship with Him. The devil isn't the primary issue—he is only taking advantage of the fact that your fellowship with God has been broken. James 4:7 has the right priorities: "Submit therefore to God. Resist the devil and he will flee from you." The primary issue is to submit to God.

Satan knows that if he can keep our minds distracted, we won't have much of a prayer life with God. Prayer is the vital link for God's guidance. If we are going to walk with God through the darkness, we must have the peace of God which surpasses all comprehension and guards our hearts and minds in Christ Jesus (Philippians 4:7). It is beyond the scope of this book to describe how that can be achieved, but I have sought to do that in my two previous books, *Victory Over the Darkness* and *The Bondage Breaker.*

Take a look at 1 John 2:12-14. "Little children" of the faith have not learned how to overcome the evil one. They are at the petition level of prayer. "Fathers" are those who have a deep experiential knowledge of God. They have known Him from the beginning (1 John 2:13). To them everything begins with God and nothing that lasts starts without Him. They walk with a personal God and they pray without ceasing. They have reached the intercession level of prayer.

We need to understand where we are in our relationship with God in order to know how to ward off the devil's schemes. An undergraduate student stopped by my office to ask some questions about Satanism. I answered some of her questions and then said, "I don't think you should be researching this." She asked, "Why not?" I answered, "Because you're not free." Surprised by my straightforwardness she said, "What do you mean by that?" I responded, "I'm sure you struggle in your devotional life, and your prayer life is probably zero. You probably have difficulty paying attention in your Bible classes, and I'm pretty sure your self-esteem is down in the mud. You may even entertain suicide thoughts." Surprised, she asked, "How do you know that?" She told her friend later, "That guy read my mind."

I didn't read her mind, but I've counseled lots of people who have not overcome the evil one. Most have not understood the battle going on for their minds and they've gotten in over their heads. I encouraged this student to take my class on spiritual conflicts and biblical counseling. After the class, she wrote me this letter:

> I guess I was expecting an emotionally moving experience. But what I've discovered this last week is a feeling of control, like my mind is my own. I haven't had my usual strung-out periods of thought and contemplation. My mind simply feels quieted.
>
> It really is a strange feeling. My emotions have been stable. I haven't felt depressed once this week. My will is mine. I feel like I have been able to choose to live my life abiding in Christ.
>
> Scripture seems different. I have a totally new perspective. I actually understand what it is saying. I feel left alone, but not in a bad way. I'm not lonely, just a single person. For the first time, I believe I actually understand what it means to be a

Christian, who Christ is and who I am in Him. I feel capable of helping people and capable of handling myself.

I've been a co-dependent for years, but this last week I haven't had the slightest feeling or need for someone. I guess I'm describing what it is like to be at peace. I feel this quiet, soft joy in my heart. I have been more friendly and comfortable with strangers. It hasn't been a struggle to get through the day. And I have been participating actively in life and not merely passively, critically watching it. Thank you for lending me your hope. I believe I have my own now in Christ.

Having overcome the evil one, she is a "young woman" in her relationship with God (1 John 2:14). Because of her mental peace, she is experiencing the guidance of God in her daily life. Finding freedom in Christ is what allows people to relate personally to God in prayer.

If you hear His voice, don't harden your heart. Deal with the issues He brings to your mind, and take every thought captive to the obedience of Christ.

If it's your desire to actively pursue God and find out just how personal He really is, would you pray with me?

Dear Heavenly Father, I want my heart sprinkled clean so I can come boldly before Your throne of grace. Forgive me for ever shutting You out of my life. Search me, O God, try me and see if there is any hurtful way in me. Lead me in an everlasting way. I want to walk in the light as You are in the light. I bring my life before You as an open book, realizing that You already know the thoughts and intentions of my heart. I trust my entire life to You. Amen.

WALKING THROUGH THE DARKNESS

The life led by the Spirit of God is marvelous. Sensing His presence, living victoriously and knowing the truth are characteristics of a free person. But what if you couldn't sense His presence? What if God, for some reason, suspended His blessings? What would you do if you were faithfully following God and suddenly all external circumstances turned sour?

Job was enjoying the benefits of living righteously when, unexpectedly, it was all taken away. Health, wealth and family—all gone! If we found ourselves in Job's shoes, our minds would spin with questions:

"What did I do to deserve this?"

"Did I miss a turn in the road?"

"Is this what I get for living a righteous life?"

"Where is God?"

"God, why are You doing this to me?"

And like Job, we may even feel like cursing the day we were born.

My family and I have been through two extremely dark periods in our lives. There were days I wasn't sure if we were going to make it. If it weren't for the message of Isaiah 50:10,11, I'm not sure we would have spiritually survived:

> Who is among you that fears the Lord, that obeys the voice of His servant, that walks in darkness and has no light? Let him trust in the name of the Lord, and rely on his God. Behold all you who kindle a fire, who encircle yourselves with firebrands, walk in the light of your fire, and among the brands you have set ablaze, this you will have from My hand, and you will lie down in torment.

Isaiah is asking if there is a believer, somebody who fears the Lord, who walks in darkness. But he is not referring to the darkness of sin, or even the darkness of this world. He is talking about the darkness of uncertainty—that blanket of heaviness that settles in as though a black cloud has drifted over our very being. The assurance of yesterday has been replaced by the uncertainties of tomorrow. God has suspended His conscious blessings. Church has become a dismal experience. Friends seem more like a bother than a blessing.

What is a person to do during these times? What's the purpose? Why would this happen to a true believer? Using Isaiah 50:10,11 as our guide, we'll look at what a Christian should and should not do when he finds himself walking through the darkness of uncertainty. And we'll discuss how God leads (and why He would lead) us down such a faith-testing path.

Never Stop

One of the most important things Isaiah tells us is that, no matter how dark it gets, we are to keep on walking.

In the light we can see the next step. The path ahead is clear. We know a friend from an enemy, and we can see where the obstacles are. But when darkness settles in, every natural instinct says to drop out, sit down, stop! We begin to doubt the truth of the Word that had been a lamp unto our feet. We become fearful of the next step.

Isaiah encourages us that, no matter how dark it gets, we are to keep on walking.

I wrote earlier about an exciting church building program where God had obviously guided us to new property and enabled the construction of new facilities. Few are the times when God so dramatically leads as He did in that situation. Usually it's more subtle and sometimes it doesn't seem like He's guiding us at all—as the months following that miracle showed me.

After the building program was finished, God released me from that pastorate. I was nearing the end of my doctoral studies and facing the major task of a dissertation. I also knew that my seminary education was not quite complete. I resigned in the summer and began one of the most difficult educational years of my life. In one year I completed forty-three semester units, seventeen of them foreign language (Greek and Hebrew). In the middle of the year I took my comprehensive exams and by the end of the year I had finished my doctoral dissertation. I also taught part-time at Talbot School of Theology. A back-breaking year to say the least.

Joanne and I started that year with the assurance that $20,000 would be made available for our use interest free. Our plan was to pay off the loan when we sold our home after I graduated and found a ministry. Upon completion of my education, I was confident God would have a place for us in His kingdom plan. So I proceeded with a great deal of anticipation of finishing my doctorate and a second master's degree. For the next six months our life unfolded as planned.

Then God turned out the light.

News came that the second half of the $20,000 wasn't going to come in. I had no job and my educational goals were only half-completed at best. I always considered myself a dependable, faithful man, but now I was on the brink of not being able to provide for the basic needs of my family. Having no other source of income, our cupboards became bare. I had been so certain of God's calling six months earlier, but now my confidence was shaken.

Everything came to a head two weeks before my comprehensive exams. Only 10 percent of the doctoral candidates had passed the previous testing, so there was a lot of pressure. If I didn't pass the exams, I couldn't start my dissertation, and I had already invested three years and $15,000 in the program. And at this point I didn't even know where my next meal would come from. I had equity in my home, but interest rates at the time were so high that houses simply weren't selling. I looked into a couple of ministry opportunities, but they weren't for me and I knew I couldn't accept them. The problem wasn't an unwillingness to work—I would have sold hotdogs to provide for my family.

I wanted God's will!

I began to wonder if I had made the wrong decision. His leading was so clear the past summer, so why all the doubts now? Why this darkness? It was as though God had dropped me into a funnel and the farther I fell, the darker it became. When I thought it couldn't get any darker, I hit the narrow part. Then at the absolute darkest hour, God dropped me out of the bottom of that funnel and everything became clear.

About 2 A.M. on a Thursday morning the dawn broke. Nothing changed circumstantially, but everything changed internally. I remember waking up and jumping up and down on the bed. My startled wife woke up and wondered what was going on, but she, too, could sense something had taken place. There was a conscious awareness of God in a remarkable way. Without audible voices or visions, God, in His quiet and gentle way, renewed my mind: *Neil, do you walk by faith or do you walk by sight? Can you walk by faith now? You believed Me last summer. Do you believe Me now? Neil, do you love Me or do you love My blessings? Do you worship Me for who I am or do you worship Me for the blessings I bring? What if I suspended My conscious presence in your life? Would you still believe in Me?*

I knew I would. In my spirit I responded, "Lord, You know I love You, and I walk by faith, not by sight. Lord, I worship You because of who You are, and I know that You will never leave me nor forsake me. Forgive me, Lord, that I ever doubted Your place in my life or questioned Your ability to provide for all our needs."

Precious moments like these can't be planned or predicted. They're never repeatable. What we have previously learned from the Bible becomes incarnate during these times. Our worship is purified and our love clarified. Faith moves from a textbook definition to a living reality. Trust is deepened when God puts us in a position where we have no other choice but to trust. We truly learn to live by faith when circumstances are not working favorably for us.

Do I need to share what happened the next day? The dean at Talbot School of Theology called to ask if I had taken another position. He asked me not to accept anything until we had the opportunity to talk. That Friday afternoon he offered me the position I've held for the past eight years.

Friday evening a man from my previous ministry stopped by at 10 P.M. When I asked him what he was doing at our home at that hour of the night, he said he wasn't sure. I invited him in with the assurance, "We'll figure out something." I half-jokingly asked him if he'd like to buy my house and he responded, "Maybe I would." The next Tuesday he and his parents made an offer on our house which we accepted. Now we could sell our house because we knew where we were headed.

Nothing had changed externally before that morning, but everything had changed internally. In a moment, God can change what circumstances can never change.

My wife and I had previously made a commitment together that helped sustain us during the hard times: We will never make a major decision when we are down. That alone has kept me from resigning after difficult board meetings or not-so-perfect messages. The point is, never doubt in darkness what God has clearly shown in the light. We are to keep on walking in the light of previous revelation. If it was true six months ago, it's still true. If we're serious about our walk with God, He will test us to determine whether we love Him or His blessings. He may cloud the future so we can learn to walk by faith and not by sight or feelings.

Understand that God has not left us; He has only suspended His conscious presence so that our faith will not rest on feelings or be established by unique experiences or blessings. Suppose when we were children our parents had found themselves in difficult financial circumstances and we didn't get any Christmas presents. Would we stop loving them? Would we stop looking to them for direction and support? Of course not.

If God's ministry of darkness should envelop you, listen to Isaiah's advice: Keep on walking.

The Consequences of Doing It Your Way

Isaiah's next piece of advice is a warning of what not to do when the way gets dark: Don't light your own fire. The natural tendency when we don't see it God's way is to do it our way. Resist the urge to create your own light.

Notice the text again: "Behold all you who kindle a fire, who encircle yourselves with firebrands, walk in the light of your fire." God is not talking about the fire of judgment; He's talking about fire that creates light. Notice what happens when people create their own light: "And among the brands you have set ablaze, this you will have from My hand, you will lie down in torment." Go ahead, do it your way. God will allow it, but misery will follow.

Let me illustrate from the Bible. God called Abraham out of Ur into the promised land. In Genesis 12, a covenant was made in which God promised Abraham that his descendants would be more numerous than the sands of the sea or the stars in the sky. Abraham lived his life in the light of that promise, then God turned out the light.

So many years passed that his wife Sarah could no longer bear a child by natural means. God's guidance had been so clear before, but now it looked like Abraham would have to assist God in its fulfillment. Who could blame Abraham for creating his own light? Sarah supplied the match by offering her handmaiden to Abraham. Out of that union came the Arab nation which has been in conflict with the Jewish nation ever since.

Moses tried to create his own light. God superintended his birth and provided for his preservation. Raised in the home of Pharaoh, Moses was given the second most prominent position in Egypt. But God had put a burden on his heart to set his people free. Impulsively Moses pulled out his sword and God turned out the light. Abandoned to the back side of the desert, Moses spent forty years tending his father-in-law's sheep. Then one day, Moses turned to see a burning bush that wasn't consumed. God had turned the light back on.

I'm not suggesting that we will have to wait forty years, but our darkness may last for weeks, months and possibly, for some exceptional people, even years. God is in control and He knows exactly how big a knothole He can pull us through. When we are stretched to our limit, He pulls us out the other side.

After the Night, the Day

Our second period of darkness occurred a number of years ago when my wife developed cataracts in both eyes and slowly lost her sight. She had two surgeries within four months, but because she couldn't have lens implants, she had to be fitted with cataract glasses and finally contacts. Five years later, technological advances allowed her to have implant surgery.

The surgery was successful, but Joanne didn't recover physically or emotionally. She became fearful, paranoid and depressed. For months she went from doctor to doctor. Because she was forty-five years old, most of the doctors wanted to declare her a head case or a hormone case. She was neither. All they could figure out to do was fill her full of tranquilizers and sleeping pills. She was hospitalized five times.

Needless to say, this whole process became exceedingly expensive. Our insurance ran out and we had to sell our house to pay the medical bills. I struggled with what my role should be in relation to my wife. Should I be her pastor, counselor or husband? I decided there was only one role I could fulfill in her life, and that was to be her husband. If someone was going to fix my wife, it would have to be someone other than myself. My role was to hold her every day and say, "Joanne, someday this will pass." I was thinking it would be a matter of a few weeks or months, but it turned into a long, fifteen-month ordeal.

During this dark time, Isaiah 21:11,12 was very meaningful to me:

> One keeps calling to me from Seir, "Watchman, how far gone is the night? Watchman, how far gone is the night?" The watchman says, "Morning comes but also night."

I base my life on the hope that morning comes. No matter how dark the night, morning comes. And it's always darkest before the dawn. At our darkest moment, I wasn't even sure if Joanne was going to make it.

We had a day of prayer at Biola University. I had nothing to do with the program other than to set aside special time for prayer in my classes. In the evening the undergraduate students had a communion service. I hadn't planned on going, but since work had detained me on campus I decided to participate. I sat on the gym floor with the undergrad students and took communion.

I'm sure nobody in the student body was aware that it was one of the loneliest times of my life. I was deeply committed to doing God's will, and I was walking as best I could in the light of previous revelation, but I felt abandoned. God had stripped my family of everything we owned. All we had left was each other and our relationship to God.

But when there was nowhere else to turn, morning came!

If God has ever spoken to my heart, He did in that communion service. It didn't come through the pastor's message or the testimonies of the students, but it did come in the context of taking communion. I suppose the essence was this: *Neil, there's a price to pay for freedom. It cost My Son His life. Are you willing to pay the price?*

"Dear God," I prayed, "if that's the reason, I'm willing. But if it's some stupid thing I'm doing, then I don't want to be a part of it anymore." I left with the inner assurance that it was over. The circumstances hadn't changed, but in my heart I knew that morning had come.

Later that week Joanne woke up one morning and said, "Neil, I slept last night." Sixteen days before, she had visited a family practice doctor who specialized in the treatment of clinical depression. He got her off the medication that had been prescribed by other doctors and treated her chemical imbalance with proper medication. On that morning she knew she was finally on the road to recovery. She never looked back and continued on to full and complete health.

Learning True Resources

You may be asking, "What's the point of the dark times? What's God trying to do? What's He trying to teach us?"

In God's ministry of darkness, we learn a lot about ourselves. Whatever was left of my old nature that gave simplistic advice such as, "Read your Bible" or "Just work harder" or "Pray more," was mercifully stripped away. Most people going through dark times would love to do the right thing, but many can't and don't know why.

In God's ministry of darkness we learn compassion. We learn to wait patiently with people. We learn to respond to the emotional needs of people who have lost hope. We weep with those who weep. We don't try to teach or instruct or advise. We had some "friends" advise us in our time of darkness, and I can tell you it hurts.

Job had friends like that. In his hour of darkness Job needed a few good friends to just sit with him. His friends did that for one week and then their patience ran out. The meaningful help Joanne and I received was from people who just stood by us and prayed.

If God took away every external blessing and reduced our assets to nothing more than meaningful relationships, would that be enough to sustain us? Yes, I believe it would.

In our case, within two years God replaced everything we lost. And this time it was far better in terms of home, family and ministry. Be encouraged: God makes everything right in the end.

Perhaps God brings us to the end of our resources so we can discover the vastness of His. We don't hear many sermons about brokenness in our churches these days, yet in all four Gospels Jesus taught us to deny ourselves, pick up our cross daily and follow Him. When it was time for the Son of Man to be glorified, He said: "Truly, truly, I say to you, unless a grain of wheat falls into the ground and dies, it remains by itself alone; but if it dies it bears much fruit" (John 12:24). I don't know any painless way to die to ourselves, but I do know that it's necessary and that it's the best possible thing that could ever happen to us: "For we who live are constantly being delivered over to death for Jesus' sake, that the life of Jesus also may be manifested in our mortal flesh" (2 Corinthians 4:11).

If we are relying on degrees, diplomas, status and self-confidence, God is going to strip that confidence away. Paul had to learn that power is perfected in weakness:

> Beloved, do not be surprised at the fiery ordeal among you which comes upon you for your testing as though some strange thing were happening to you. But to the degree that you share the sufferings of Christ, keep on rejoicing, so that also at the revelation of His glory you may rejoice with exultation (1 Peter 4:12).

We need the attitude of the early church, who rejoiced because they were considered worthy to suffer shame for His name (Acts 5:41). Are we afraid of the truth in 2 Timothy 3:12: "And indeed all who desire to live Godly in Christ Jesus will suffer"?

"No pain, no gain," says the body builder. Isn't that true in the spiritual realm as well? "All discipline for the moment seems not to be joyful, but sorrowful; yet to those who have been trained by it, afterwards it yields the peaceful fruit of righteousness" (Hebrews 12:11). Proven character comes from persevering through the tribulations of life (Romans 5:3-5).

Maybe the ultimate purpose of walking in darkness is to learn to trust in the Lord. Isaiah says, "Let him trust in the name of the Lord and rely upon His name" (Isaiah 50:10). Every great period of personal growth in my life and ministry has been preceded by a major time of testing.

Learning to Wait

Possibly the greatest sign of spiritual maturity is the ability to postpone rewards. The ultimate test would be to receive nothing in this lifetime, but to look forward to receiving our reward in the life to come. The writer of Hebrews expresses it this way:

> All these died in faith without receiving the promises, but having seen them and having welcomed them from a distance and having confessed that they were strangers and exiles on this earth, for those who say such things, make it clear that they

are seeking a country of their own. . . . And all these having gained approval through their faith did not receive what was promised because God had provided something better for us, so that apart from us they should not be made perfect (Hebrews 11:13,39).

If I had known beforehand what my family would have to go through to get where we are today, I probably wouldn't have come. But looking back, we all say, "We're glad we came." Remember, God makes everything right in the end, though it may not even be in this lifetime. I believe with all my heart that when life is done and we're looking back, we will be able to say that the will of God is good, acceptable and perfect.

It is not the critic who counts, nor the man who points how the strong man stumbled, or where the doer of deeds could have done better. The credit belongs to the man who is actually in the arena, whose face is marred by the dust and sweat and blood; who strives valiantly; who errs and comes short again and again; who knows the great enthusiasms, the great devotions, and spends himself in a worthy cause; who, at best, knows in the end the triumph of high achievement; and who, at the worst, if he fails, at least fails while daring greatly, so that his place shall never be with those cold and timid souls who know neither victory or defeat.
                                          —Theodore Roosevelt

We may be in the arena, but we don't have to fear the outcome of the battle. I can say that with confidence. The battle is not ours; it is the Lord's. We have His truth and He has made every provision for us. Satan has no place in our lives. The Holy Spirit will guide us in the continuing experience of God's will for our lives.

I will not close this chapter as I have done before with a suggested prayer. Instead, it is just my prayer that your heart will be filled with words that you would now want to express to your Lord—words of praise, words of pain, words of commitment, words about knowing God's truth and His will in the New Age.

Would you now pray?

Notes

Chapter 3

1. Martin Wells Knapp, *Impressions* (Wheaton, IL: Tyndale House Publishers, 1984), p. 32.
2. Knapp, *Impressions*, p. 43.
3. Knapp, *Impressions*, p. 14.

Chapter 4

1. For the serious student who would like to know the biblical place for prophecy and its use in the church today, I suggest *Showing the Spirit* by D. A. Carson (Grand Rapids, MI: Baker Book House, 1987).

For information concerning resources and schedule of Dr. Neil T. Anderson's ministry, please write:

Freedom in Christ Ministries
491 E. Lambert Road
La Habra, CA 90631

Walking in the Light

Chapter 1: Can We Really Know?

1. Why is discovering the will of God for our lives such a mystery? Now personalize it—why do you sometimes wonder what the will of God is for your life?

2. When looking for guidance in making key decisions for their lives, where do many people turn for help? *See pages. 9 & 10.*

3. Why do some Christians go to other believers for help in making personal decisions?

4 What two reasons does the author give for not needing to go to someone more "spiritual" to discover God's will for our lives? *Page 10.*

5. What experiences in your life indicate that God has been preparing you for what you are doing now?

6. Dr. Anderson shares personal experiences on pages 10 and 11 as illustrations of how God leads and shapes our

lives. Can you identify a similar pattern in your life, or that of a close friend?

7.   According to 1 Timothy 4:1, why can we be misled?

8.   What is the danger the author highlights in discussing our technological age? *Page 13.*

9.   In what ways can we open ourselves to deceiving spirits? *Pages 11 & 12.*

10. After reading this chapter, describe what kind of help you expect to get from this book to help you discover the will of God.

Chapter 2: Rationalism Versus Mysticism

1. What are two ways of looking at life and God that are contrary to the Word of God, yet are thriving in America today?

2. What happens when we leave God out of the picture? *Page 18.* What evidence of this do you see in our society?

3. What are two sides of the same coin in the Western mindset? *Page 18.* How does the dictionary define the two words the author uses?

4. Why is the scientific method inadequate in trying to discover God? *Page 19.*

5. What are the six unifying factors in New Age thinking? *Pages 22 - 24.*

6. Since monism is so much a part of New Age philosophy, describe why this thought system is inadequate in trying to understand God. *Page 22.*

7. How does pantheism manifest itself in New Age doctrine? *Pages 22 & 23.*

8. What are the counterfeit elements in the belief in a change of consciousness? *Page 23.*

9. What are the key elements in cosmic evolutionary optimism? *Page 23.*

10. Where does the idea that we can change reality by what we believe show up in our society? *Page 23.*

11. What makes channeling and the use of mediums so attractive, even to some Christians? *Page 24.*

12. Where and when do we find real wisdom and power?
    Page 25.

13. Without Christ, what happens to people who are cognitive, materialistic only, people? *Page 26.*

14. Without Christ, what happens to intuitive, feeling only, people? *Page 26.*

15. How do we achieve a balance between rational thinking, relationship and intuitive type approaches? *Page 27.*

16. With what kind of thinking do you identify—and what do you now see as a danger in your life?

Chapter 3: Deceiving Spirits

1. In what ways can believers be led astray by ideas that enter their minds? *Pages 29 - 31.*

2. What is the tension we experience, the battle going on in our minds, according to the author and 1 Timothy 4:1? *Page 30.*

3. What is the greatest, most obvious, symptom of demonic activity in both believers and unbelievers? *Page 31.*

4. According to the author, what is the greatest determinant of mental health in the believer? *Page 31.*

5. What is the greatest determinant of mental illness? *Page 32.*

6. What is the area in which Satan attacks us, and what is the thrust of his attack? *Page 32.*

7. What is Satan's tactic as our accuser—and what is his greatest strategy? *Page 33.*

8. What is the doorway Satan uses to gain access to our minds and feelings? *Page 34.* As you examine yourself, do you sense you are providing an open doorway to Satan's lies by your attitude? What do you need to do to close that doorway?

9. How can we help people gain freedom from the control of Satan? *Page 35.*

10. What does the author mean when he urges the reader to "choose truth"? *Page 36.* What specific strategy does the author recommend as part of this process?

11. Write out your own prayer in response to what you have learned about how Satan is influencing your thinking and feelings about yourself.

Chapter 4: False Prophets

1. Which group do you most closely identify with, those who believe God no longer manifests Himself in the miraculous or those who look for supernatural manifestations of God in every worship service?

2. Having identified your position, what might be a weakness or danger in it? *Page 40.*

3. What is our present position as believers, according to Ephesians 2:19-22 and Colossians 1:13? *Page 41.*

4. On what basis were Old Testament men of God recognized as prophets? As a result, what was the test of a true prophet? *Pages 41 & 42.*

5. How can we today differentiate between the position of a prophet and the gift of prophecy? *Pages 42 – 43.*

6. What are some modern examples of people posing as prophets of God, when in reality they are false prophets? *Pages 44 & 46.*

7. What is a key function of a true prophecy? *Page 47.*

8. How can we determine the credibility of a contemporary prophet? *Pages 47 & 48.*

9. What are three identifiers of false prophets? *Pages 47 - 49.*

10. What are key cautions when guarding against false prophets? *Page 49.*

11. According to the author, what is our responsibility in relation to the gifts of the Spirit? *Page 51.*

12. According to the author, what would happen if the gift of prophecy were used properly in the church? *Page 51.*

13. How can we determine if there is a misuse of prophecy in the church? *Page 51.*

14. Review the five tests for evaluating prophetic utterances. If you are involved in giving or receiving prophetic utterances, how do these measure up to this five-fold test? *Page 52.*

Chapter 5: Facing Fear

1. What was Jesus' most frequent admonition when interacting with His disciples and those He spoke to? *Page 56.*

2. What is the fear controlling part or all of your life? Identify where it came from and describe how it affects you.

3. What are two key characteristics or attributes of genuine fear? *Pages 56 & 57.*

4. Based on the author's descriptions, is the fear you described earlier a legitimate fear or a phobia?

5. Are phobias, or irrational fears, any less real than legitimate fears? Why or why not?

6. How can God help us with our fear of a person? *Pages 58 & 59.* Describe an experience where you received relief from the fear of a person.

7. Although death is universally feared, why don't we as Christians need to fear death? *Page 60.*

8. According to the author, how does Satan seek to intimidate us and create fear in our minds? *Pages 60 & 61.*

9. What approach helps us overcome demonic forces in other people when we are confronted by them? *Pages 62 & 63.*

10. The author says fear can usurp God's place in your life. Does the fear you described earlier tend to crowd God out of your life? If so, describe how that happens.

11. Consider again the fear you identified earlier. Now complete the Phobia Finder on page 68. Then go back to Question 4 and see how the results agree with the answer you gave there.

Chapter 6: The Essential Prerequisite

1. According to Jesus, what is the essential prerequisite to knowing the will of God? *Page 71.*

2. Why did we come into this world without God's presence in our lives and without the knowledge of His ways? *Page 72.*

3. Where do we normally seek our identity and purpose for our lives? *Page 72 and Ephesians 2:1-3.*

4. How do we know Satan has been disarmed? *Page 73 and Colossians 2:13-15.*

5. What constitutes the "flesh" in our walk as believers, according to the author? How do we deal with this "learned independence"? *Page 74.*

6. What is the will of God for every believer, according to 1 Thessalonians 4:3?

7. What is the primary focus of God's will for us today? *Page 76.*

8. How can you make the most of every opportunity to "bloom where you are planted," thus fulfilling the will of God at present? *Pages 76 – 78.* List three opportunities that you know you could take in your neighborhood; in your church; in your town or city.

9. Why does God's leading sometimes not make sense? *Page 79.* Describe an experience that illustrates this.

10. What does the author mean by "abandonment to the will of God"? *Page 80.* What could that mean in your life today—and how would it affect how you live tomorrow?

Chapter 7: Glorifying God

1. What is the essential prerequisite to knowing the will of God, according to John 7:17? If the number 0 is unwillingness to meet that precondition, and 5 is total commitment to fulfilling that precondition, how would you rate yourself on the scale below?

    0   1   2   3   4   5

2. What will we be ignorant of if we question or reject the will of God? *Page 83.*

3. What is the second precondition to knowing the will of God—beyond being willing to do it? *Pages 84 & 85.* How close to this precondition do you rate your motive on the scale below, with 5 indicating you are meeting the biblical motivation?

    0   1   2   3   4   5

4. Do you feel a desperate need for affirmation? Is a hurtful experience in the past clouding your experience of God's will? How can you deal with this in the light of the author's examples on pages 85 to 88?

5. If you feel that God is a vengeful, angry God, how will this color your response to God?

6. If you see God as a loving Father, how will this affect your response to God?

7. In what ways have you been bringing glory to God in your life?

8. How does God's teaching on right behavior differ from the

world's attitudes? *Pages 89 & 90.* Rate yourself on the scale
below, with number 5 indicating the desirable attitude.

a. I am truly submissive to God   0 1 2 3 4 5
b. I am submissive to my boss   0 1 2 3 4 5
c. I am submissive to my husband   0 1 2 3 4 5
d. I demonstrate a submissive   0 1 2 3 4 5
    spirit to my wife

9. What is your heart response to the Scriptures presented on
being "In Christ" on pages 91 to 93? If your heart is still dis-
agreeing with what your head tells you to be true according
to the Bible, re-read the passages and repeat aloud what
they teach.

Chapter 8: A Light to My Path

1. According to the author, how do we sometimes get our own way? *Page 95.*

2. In what ways may your church exhibit some of the same attitudes as the Jewish community at the time of Christ? *See Mark 7:9.*

3. What can we learn from the examples of King Ahaziah about seeking help from spirits and mediums? *Page 97.*

4. What two factors prevent us from getting a true perspective on God's Word and what the Holy Spirit is trying to teach us? *Page 98.*

5. If married, analyze your relationship with your spouse in comparison to the author's description of levels of maturity in marriage on page 99.

6. How do you react to the author's description of theological biases? What has been your personal bias, and how does it affect your relationship with others? *Page 99.*

7. Review the four principles of a grammatical, historical method of biblical interpretation. Which ones have provided significant insight for you in helping you better understand the Bible?

8. Which of the five hindrances presented by the author on pages 101 and 102 are creating the biggest barrier for your understanding and applying the Word of God to your life?

9. Why is change in a church often so extremely difficult? Are you one of those opposed to change, or are you ready to become a "new wineskin" in the church?

10. What is the key conclusion presented in the last paragraph under point number one on page 105?

11. If you are part of a church group, describe its purpose in one sentence. If you cannot do that, ask yourself why you are part of the group. In addition, consider asking the leadership of the group what the group's purpose is.

12. The author writes, "The ones who have a real Christian experience are the ones who are free to change their Christian practices." Do you fit that description? If not, what steps do you need to take?

13. What do you consider the old wine of your life? the new wine of your life in the church? *See number 4 on page 111.*

14. Examine your experience in your group or church, answering the following questions honestly: Is it real? Does it relate? Does it unify?

Chapter 9: A Peace in My Heart

1. Why does the light from the Lamp of the Word of God decrease and dim when we fail to acknowledge our limited perspective as humans?

2. What are two traits that characterize people who are false prophets, according to 2 Peter 2:10?

3. Yet what are the standards by which we tend to judge leaders? *Page 115.*

4. Which of the ways that people use to find peace are you employing at this time? *Page 116.*

5. Why does the person trying to control people and environment not achieve peace? *Page 117.*

6. What do we need to "order" if we want to achieve peace for a troubled mind? *Page 117.*

7. How can we gain "more healthiness and simple, unaffected goodness"? *Pages 117 - 119.*

8. What does a materialist struggle with? a doubter? And what is the root issue for both? *Page 119.*

9. Identify something you are anxious about and work your way through the "Anxiety Worksheet" on page 123.

10. Which truth helped crack open the door to inner peace, a door locked by either a strong focus on material goods or a failure to trust the Lord to provide?

Chapter 10: Sanctified Common Sense

1. If we are always looking for a sign from God to guide us, what are we forgetting about how God works in His universe?

2. According to the author, what is most impressive about how God works in our life? *Page 127.* Do you agree or disagree with the author, and why?

3. If we put the Lord to the test to achieve our own goals, why may God choose not to respond to us? *Page 127 and Matthew 4:7.*

4. Who does scripture primarily associate with signs and wonders in the last days—Holy Spirit-directed believers or false prophets? *Page 128.*

5. According to Jesus in John 13:35, what is the distinguishing characteristic of the true disciple?

6. Describe the difference between biblical wisdom and Western rationalism. *Page 129.*

7. Write out your response to the author's question,"If you are striving to please men, who are you a bond-servant of?" Let it reflect your own life situation.

8. What is the basic problem with trying to determine God's will by using the "fleece"? *Page 131.* Does God ever respond to our weakness when we use a fleece?

9. Why are circumstances an unreliable guide to making important decisions?

10. Why do we have to carefully weigh the counsel of godly friends? *Page 133.*

11. Is there any evidence in your life that God has guided you in keeping with your gifts and talents? Give some examples.

12. The author provides several examples of how God changed his desires. Reflect on how God has changed your desires over the years, or describe how He has changed a friend's desires.

13. Are you faced with a key decision? Take the ten-step decision-making test on page 140. Then write down what conclusion you reached as you worked your way through the issues raised.

Chapter 11: The Life of Faith

1. Describe an area in your life or life situation that illustrates the key prerequisite for ministry presented in 1 Timothy 1:12.

2. If 1 Timothy 1:12 is really true, why is it so difficult to find Sunday school teachers and youth sponsors who will give more than six weeks to three months of service? Why are we living as Proverbs 20:6 describes?

3. List some ways in which you demonstrate everyday faith on a daily basis.

4. According to the author, what is a form of religious self-hypnosis? *Page 143.*

5. Why do we have so much difficulty accepting the reality of the invisible in today's world? *Page 144.*

6. What determines our level of faith in God? What role does obedience have in increasing faith? *Page 147.*

7. Highlight the definition of what a miracle is, as given on page 148—or write it out as a reminder.

8. Illustrate from your own life, or that of a friend, the author's words, "The will of God never leads us where the grace of God cannot enable us."

9. If you are facing a key decision, what is God saying to you through Philippians 4:13?

10. What action do you need to take if you are to live in faith obedience, according to 1 John 3:16-18?

11. According to the author, what is the primary purpose of speaking what we believe? *Page 152.*

12. How do we gain assurance we have not been taken in by Satan's lies when beginning to move forward in faith? *See 1 John 4:1– 4; 5:4– 5.*

13. In what areas of your life do you need to develop your faith walk and faith words?

Chapter 12: Spiritual Discernment

1. How does the principle provided in 1 John 3:7–8 protect us when we need to exercise spiritual discernment?

2. Jesus was able to discern what was in the hearts of men and women. Since the Holy Spirit lives in us, should Christians have a special level of discernment as well? Or is it the right of only a few? *Pages 158 – 160.*

3. How does a true shepherd leader in the church exercise spiritual leadership? *Page 159.*

4. What are the five conclusions the author draws from 1 Corinthians 2:9-16 on how the Holy Spirit provides discernment? *Page 161.*

5. How is the mind like a computer—and why is this "computer" still programmed to live independently of God? In other words, why do we need our minds renewed even though we're Christians? *Pages 162 & 163.*

6. On what plane or level does spiritual discernment manifest itself? *Page 165.*

7. What are the conditions for a Christian to have spiritual discernment? *Pages 167 & 168.*

8. What are the characteristics of deceiving spirits? *Page 168.*

9. Our ability to discern grows in proportion to several areas of knowledge and maturity. What are they? *Page 168.*

10. Have you ever sensed an ability to discern the presence of evil beings in other persons? What did you do about it? How can you increase your ability to distinguish between good and evil? *Pages 168 & 169.*

Chapter 13: Walking by the Spirit

1. What were the three key elements ensuring the safe landing
    of the young pilot in the author's opening illustration?

    a. Confidence in _____

    b. Knowledge of_____

    c. Faith in _____

    Now insert what elements we as Christians need to have
    for a similar "safe landing" as believers.

2. How did the early church discover the mind of Christ?
    Page 174.

3. Why has preaching morality not changed our society into
    an obedient, God-fearing community? *Pages 174 & 175.* If
    you disagree with the author, what examples can you
    provide to buttress your argument?

4. What kind of freedom is the apostle Paul writing about in
    Galatians 5:13? What are some of the excesses we see today
    among those who consider the freedom of Christ a license
    to do whatever they want?

5. Why does a legalistic approach to the Christian life not change
    the inside of man, his attitudes and motivation? *Pages 177 & 178.*

6. The author writes, "The law . . . can stimulate the desire to
    do that which it tries to prohibit," and provides an example.
    Page 179. What are some of the things you have been told are
    wrong, but which you still desire to do?

7. Re-read the author's comparison of the Christian life to a
    journey down a road *(see bottom of page 179)*. Which side
    of the road presents the most danger to you, based on your

training and personal inclinations? How can you stay in the center of the road?

8. If we walked with Jesus rather than striking out on our own ways, what would we learn? *See bottom of page 181.*

9. What is the most attractive part about Jesus as you read the description of Him in Matthew 11:28-30?

10. How does the Holy Spirit's guidance come according to the author? *Pages 182 & 183.*

11. After working through this chapter, what steps can you take to be more attuned to the Holy Spirit's guidance in your life?

Chapter 14: Walking in the Light

1. Write down your honest responses as you read the author's account of his personal experiences with prayer. This will identify areas of inadequacy and surface feelings you may have denied up to now, establishing a basis for growth in your appreciation for and experience of prayer.

2. List reasons why you find prayer so difficult in your personal life; with your spouse; in small groups or ministry settings.

3. Read the Scripture verses cited by the author on pages 187 to 188, highlighting or writing down what the writers of these Scriptures were thankful for.

4. Why does an attitude of thanksgiving open our hearts to hearing God's voice? *Page 188.*

5. The author asserts that there is one prayer that God the Father will always answer. What is that prayer? *Page 189.* Why is that such an encouraging thought?

6. How did the author, and thus how can we, take every thought captive for Jesus Christ during our prayer time?

7. What could happen if we instead passively listen to our thoughts, according to 1 Timothy 4:1?

8. What happens when we stop trying to hide our human frailty in our communion with God? *Page 190.*

9. Why can we be open with our heavenly Father without feeling condemned by Him? *Page 191.*

10. Why is God not interested in our describing our own kingdom building to Him? *Page 191.*

11. Describe your personal experience of the three levels of prayer identified by the author: petition, personal, true intercession.

12. What process will help you deal with tempting thoughts, according to the author? *Page 194.*

13. Re-read the author's description of his forty-five-minute challenge on page 190. Then take a "walk with God" with a Bible and a pad of paper to write down what comes to mind.

Chapter 15: Walking Through the Darkness

1. What are the three characteristics of a free person, according to the author? *Page 197.*

2. If you have recently or are now going through a "Job" experience, what have been your feelings about it?

3. If the assurances of yesterday have been replaced by the uncertainties of today, how can you get back to the assurances of God? *Page 198.*

4. What principle for living did you pick up for yourself as you read the author's experience on pages 199 to 201?

5. How can you apply in your life the following: "Never doubt in darkness what God has clearly shown in the light. We are to keep on walking in the light of previous revelation"?

6. What may be some of the consequences of doing things our way, based on the experiences of Abraham and Moses? *Page 202.*

7. If you are going through an experience of "night," what do you have to look forward to, based on the author's experiences? *Pages 203 & 204.*

8. What is the most important lesson God wants to teach us during dark times? *Page 205.*

9. If God were to take away all your assets and leave you with only relationships, what relationships could sustain you?

10. If the "greatest sign of spiritual maturity is the ability to postpone rewards," how would you rate yourself on the scale below, with 5 the ability to postpone rewards?

    0　1　2　3　4　5

11. What is the confidence we have as we face the battle?

Freedom in Christ Ministries

Purpose: *Freedom in Christ Ministries is an interdenomiational, international, Bible-teaching Church ministry which exists to glorify God by equipping churches and mission groups, enabling them to fulfill their mission of establishing people free in Christ.*

Freedom in Christ Ministries offers a number of valuable video, audio, and print resources that will help both those in need and those who counsel. Among the topics covered are:

Resolving Personal Conflicts

Search for Identity ■ *Walking by Faith* ■ *Faith Renewal* ■ *Renewing the Mind* ■ *Battle for the Mind* ■ *Emotions* ■ *Relationships* ■ *Forgiveness*

Resolving Spiritual Conflicts

Position of Believer ■ *Authority* ■ *Protection* ■ *Vulnerability* ■ *Temptation* ■ *Accusation* ■ *Deception & Discernment* ■ *Steps to Freedom*

Spiritual Conflicts and Biblical Counseling

Biblical Integration ■ *Theological Basis* ■ *Walking by the Spirit* ■ *Surviving the Crisis* ■ *The Process of Growth* ■ *Counseling and Christ* ■ *Counseling the Spiritually Afflicted* ■ *Ritual Abuse*

The Seduction of Our Children

God's Answer ■ *Identity and Self-Worth* ■ *Styles of Communication* ■ *Discipline* ■ *Spiritual Conflicts and Prayer* ■ *Steps to Freedom*

Resolving Spiritual Conflicts and Cross-Cultural Ministry
Dr. Timothy Warner

Worldview Problems ■ *Warfare Relationships* ■ *Christians and Demons* ■ *The Missionary Under Attack* ■ *Practical Application for Missionaries* ■ *Steps to Freedom in Christ*

More books from Neil Anderson to help you
and those you love find freedom in Christ.

- *WALKING IN THE LIGHT*

- *RELEASED FROM BONDAGE*

- *THE BONDAGE BREAKER*

- *THE BONDAGE BREAKER STUDY GUIDE*

- *VICTORY OVER THE DARKNESS*

- *SPIRITUAL WARFARE*
  (Timothy M. Warner)

- *THE SEDUCTION OF OUR CHILDREN*

- *BREAKING THROUGH TO SPIRITUAL MATURITY*

- *LIVING FREE IN CHRIST*

- *WINNING SPIRITUAL WARFARE*

To find out more, please write or call us at
FREEDOM IN CHRIST MINISTRIES
491 E. Lambert Road, La Habra, California 90631
Phone (310) 691-9128 • FAX (310) 691-4035